The Measurement
of Portfolio
Risk Exposure

The Measurement of Portfolio Risk Exposure

Use of the Beta Coefficient

Frank B. Campanella
School of Management
Boston College

Lexington Books
D.C. Heath and Company
Lexington, Massachusetts
Toronto   London

Dedicated to

Jan
Kathleen
Patricia
Maureen

Table of Contents

List of Figures

List of Tables

Foreword

The pioneering work of Harry Markowitz in the application of statistical decision analysis techniques to portfolio management was widely acclaimed in the academic community soon after its development in the mid 1950s, but it was more than a decade before any noticeable amount of interest was stimulated among practicing professional portfolio managers and their clients. There are, no doubt, a number of reasons for this time lag, only one of which is the number of originally, and in many cases as yet, unsolved problems in the implementation of these portfolio management methods. But, by contrast, during the latter part of the last decade, these portfolio management concepts enjoyed a dramatic increase in acceptance among practitioners.

One of the ironies of this upsurge in interest on the part of portfolio managers and their clients has been that it has focused primarily on performance evaluation, whereas Markowitz's original work, and much of the research it stimulated, was aimed at portfolio selection decisions and only indirectly bore on performance measurement and evaluation. It appears that the rapid growth of the financial assets controlled and managed by institutional investors, especially pension funds and open-end mutual funds, has generated a demand for realistic and comprehensive standards for judging investment performance. Perhaps, too, the adverse investment experience of many managed pools of money, particularly those under the control of performance-oriented investment managers, in the 1969–1970 bear market made clear the important role of risk in specifying the objectives of a portfolio and in measuring its investment performance.

There have been developed in recent years a number of performance evaluation techniques which account systematically for the risk to which a portfolio was exposed as well as the return it achieved. Perhaps the most comprehensive research in this area is contained in the Bank Administration Institute's monograph *Measuring the Investment Performance of Pension Funds,* which, despite its title, raises issues and suggests procedures that are applicable to a wide range of managed investment portfolios. In this study the authors discuss a number of problems inherent in comparing performance among funds and argue, persuasively in my view, that it is essential that the yardstick against which a fund's performance is judged should itself be adjusted to reflect the same level of risk as does the fund.

Professor Campanella's research reported in this study represents a contribution to the developing field of portfolio risk measurement. To date many of the techniques developed in this field have shared the assumption that a managed portfolio's risk level remains constant over substantial periods of time and in the face of changing market environments. While this assumption may to a considerable extent be valid in the case of individual securities, it is far more tenuous for a managed portfolio whose manager is likely to change the portfolio in order to adjust its risk exposure as his view of the market environment changes. The model proposed by Professor Campanella in this study, while assuming that a security's risk remains relatively stable over time, explicitly allows for changes in the risk level of a managed portfolio and produces a portfolio risk measure that responds instantaneously to changes in portfolio composition.

Because this model is capable of reflecting shifts in a portfolio's risk level which result, at least in part, from the manager's conscious decisions, it is possible to obtain some empirical evidence on the extent to which the portfolio manager's adjustments in portfolio risk were appropriate to evolving market conditions and, at least inferentially, on how well he was able to forecast market movements. This study contains a considerable amount of interesting and revealing evidence on these issues. It also reports some empirical findings on the validity of the assumption that the risk level of an individual security is stable over time, an assumption underlying the model used to measure portfolio risk.

An interesting consequence of the development of portfolio performance evaluation technology is that this work has stimulated further initiatives in the area of portfolio selection methods. By throwing light on those dimensions of a portfolio which are essential to the evaluation process, performance measurement models have stimulated construction of portfolio management techniques designed to help achieve outstanding performance. In this context Professor Campanella suggests how his model can be used by a portfolio manager not only to gauge the level of risk his portfolio has assumed, but also to measure the impact on both risk and potential return of the portfolio decisions he has under consideration.

The original version of this study was contained in Professor Campanella's doctoral dissertation, written at the Harvard Business School under the supervision of a committee composed of Professors Eli Shapiro, William White, and myself. Partial financial support for this research was provided by a grant from the Cambridge Project, a Massachusetts Institute of Technology research project whose purpose is to develop modelling and research tools for behavioral and social science research.

Robert R. Glauber
Associate Professor,
Harvard Business School

Boston, Massachusetts
September 13, 1971

Preface

The rapid growth of the financial assets, controlled and managed by institutional investors, especially pension funds and open-end investment trusts, has generated a demand for realistic standards for judging portfolio performance. Ideally these standards should be theoretically sound, applicable in practice, and acceptable to those whose performance is being evaluated. It is the purpose of this research to develop and test such standards.

In recent years considerable effort has been devoted to this problem. Many measures of performance have been devised and applied to managed portfolios. By far the most significant problems encountered and the most significant contributions made have been in the area of risk measurement. While existing risk measures have a sound basis in theory, they are limited in two major respects. First they are inflexible. The risk level of a portfolio is assumed to remain constant or nearly constant over time. This is an unrealistic assumption for managed portfolios, where the manager can be expected to adjust portfolio risk exposure in anticipation of market changes. The second limitation is the lack of acceptance by practicing portfolio managers.

The primary purpose of this work is to develop and test a model for measuring the risk exposure of managed portfolios of common stock. The most prominent characteristic of the model proposed is its ability to generate a measure of risk that responds instantaneously to changes in portfolio composition. This quality will allow a portfolio manager to simulate portfolio transactions and assess the effects of a wide range of alternative courses of action on the risk level of the portfolio. Conversely, the model can be used internally by the fund management (or externally by prospective investors) to evaluate a portfolio manager's ability to anticipate changes in overall market level.

A secondary purpose of this study is to use the model to assess the validity of the assumption, made implicitly in research conducted to date, that portfolio volatility is stationary or nearly stationary over time.

And finally, since the proposed measure has its basis in the "market model" I have reported on a number of empirical tests conducted to examine the applicability of this model.

I find it all too infrequent that I have the occasion to acknowledge in a public and permanent way the efforts of all who have provided me with help and support. In the space of the few lines allotted here I shall attempt, albeit inadequately, to recognize some of the people who have given of themselves for my benefit in the writing of this book.

The original idea for this work was conceived in the Spring of 1968 at the Harvard Business School, during a doctoral seminar conducted by Professor Robert Glauber. A pilot study was conducted at that time. Since then, the project was kept alive and growing only because of Bob's frequent encouragement and many helpful suggestions. No less acknowledgement is due Professors Eli Shapiro, William White, and Robert S. Carlson, also members of the Harvard Business School faculty.

The task of coding and key punching the 113,000 separate items required for the research presented in Chapter 7 appeared as a monumental, if not impossible, task in the Fall of 1969. The job was done with incredible effectiveness and efficiency however, by Maurice (Mo) Monette, Ron Miller, Terry Reilly, Norm Patry, Marta de la Torre, and Ann Lally.

Key punching and verifying was accomplished quite skillfully at the Harvard Business School under the guidance of Anna Stefanakis. And a note of thanks is due Mary Sheron of Vickers Associates for her efforts in securing vast amounts of portfolio data from the Vickers archives.

A separate acknowledgement is due Linda O'Connor who typed and retyped the final manuscript. While her secretarial skill is self-evident within these pages, her diligence and patience are not, and are gratefully recognized here.

A further source of vital support was the joy provided by three young daughters. And most importantly, I would like to give a personal acknowledgement to my wife, Jan, for her unselfish understanding and continuous encouragement during the many months required to conduct this research.

While it was the support of these many that made this book possible, its organization, findings, and shortcomings are uniquely mine.

1 Introduction

The rapid growth of the financial assets controlled and managed by institutional investors, especially pension funds and open-end investment trusts, has generated a demand for realistic standards for judging portfolio performance. Ideally these standards should be theoretically sound, applicable in practice, and acceptable to those whose performance is being evaluated. It is the purpose of this work to report on the development and testing of a model that will provide the basis for one such standard.

A newspaper report of a recent mutual-fund conference highlights the nature of the need for appropriate standards of investment performance.

John C. Bogle, a leading mutual-fund executive and chairman of the industry's principal trade association, charged yesterday [that] emphasis on a "one-number" approach to measuring performance had proved unfortunate. One result has been that a trend toward broader gauges of success has already begun, he added.

In the nineteen-sixties, the president of the Wellington Management Company declared, performance meant maximum gain in rising markets. In the nineteen-seventies, it will mean optimum efficiency in all types of markets.

"The one-number approach—total percentage gain in a year, or in five or ten years—too frequently ignored such fundamental concepts of evaluating investment management as the objectives of a fund, its character and philosophy, its size, the way the results were achieved, and—most importantly—the risks that were assumed," Mr. Bogle said.

. . .

"Investors in the nineteen-seventies must be made more aware of the risk-reward equation and the concept of volatility. If they are willing to accept high risk—philosophically and psychologically, to say nothing of financially—there is every reason to expect exceptionally long-term rewards from the more aggressive funds. . . ."[1]

In recent years considerable effort has been devoted to this problem. Many measures of performance have been devised and applied to managed portfolios. By far the most significant problems encountered and the most significant contributions made, have been in the area of risk measurement. If we admit a risk-averse investor—i.e., one who expects higher rates of return for investing in

---

[1]Robert D. Hershey, Jr., "Mutual Fund Chief Sees Change," *New York Times,* April 1, 1970, pp. 61, 70.

1

assets whose returns are uncertain than for investing in assets where returns are assured—then portfolios can no longer be compared solely on a rate-of-return basis. Nor can individual portfolio returns be compared simply with a market index since the market portfolio, in all likelihood, has very different risk characteristics than the portfolio in question.

While existing risk measures have a sound basis in theory, they are limited in two major respects. First they are inflexible. The risk level of a portfolio is assumed to remain constant or nearly constant over time.[2] This is an unrealistic assumption for managed portfolios, where the manager can be expected to adjust portfolio risk exposure in anticipation of market changes. The second limitation is the lack of acceptance by practicing portfolio managers. This is, no doubt, due in part to the inflexibility noted above. But more importantly, it is perhaps due to a lack of experience with, or "feel" for the particular measures of risk employed. The more common measures now available are just not geared for the day-to-day management of a portfolio. Nor are they likely to be accepted by the portfolio manager as meaningful for the purpose of measuring his performance.

Perhaps a final reason for the lack of acceptance of risk measures proposed to date is that they attempt to measure risk in an ex-post sense. Risk is an ex-ante concept, i.e., it is concerned with future uncertainty. Empirically it is most difficult, if not impossible, to collect data relevant to portfolio managers' estimates of the future. Investment performance is measured after the fact and risk is properly determined before the fact. Risk-adjusted measures of performance therefore must rely on some type of permissive assumption in order to exist in any form. The most common assumption made is that investors in fact realize what they expected, or ex-post observations are the equivalent of ex-ante expectations.

Purpose of Research

The primary purpose of this work is to develop and test a model for measuring the risk exposure of managed portfolios of common stock. The most prominent characteristic of the model proposed is its ability to generate a measure of risk that responds instantaneously to changes in portfolio composition. This quality will allow a portfolio manager to simulate portfolio transactions and assess the effects of a wide range of alternative courses of action on the risk level of the portfolio. Conversely, the model can be used internally by

---

[2] See, for example, John Lintner, "Security Prices, Risk and Maximal Gains from Diversification," *Journal of Finance* XX, no. 4 (December 1965): 587–616; William F. Sharpe, "Mutual Fund Performance," *Journal of Business* XXXIX, no. 1, pt. II (January 1966): 119–138; Jack L. Treynor, "How to Rate Management of Investment Funds," *Harvard Business Review* XLIII (January-February 1965): 63–75; Irwin Friend, Marshall Blume, and Jean Crockett, *Mutual Funds and Other Institutional Investors: A New Perspective* (New York: McGraw Hill, 1970).

the fund management (or externally by prospective investors) to evaluate a port-folio manager's ability to anticipate changes in overall market level.

A secondary purpose of this study is to use the model to assess the validity of the assumption, made in research conducted to date, that portfolio volatility is stationary or nearly stationary over time.

Since the proposed measure has its basis in the "market model," we will also test empirically some of the assumptions implicit in the use of this particular model.[3]

Organization of the Study

Chapter 2 examines the work accomplished to date in the areas of portfolio theory, measurement of risk, and the establishment of performance criteria. It traces the historical development of portfolio theory especially as it relates to risk and performance measurement and places this research in the context of the current state of the art.

Chapters 3 and 4 are concerned with the market model. Chapter 3 examines the sensitivity of the parameters of the model to various assumptions made concerning horizon time and differencing interval. It tests the stationarity of the parameters and reports on some interesting sidelights. It also associates the results with the published findings of related research. Chapter 4 tests the specific assumption of the market model concerning the conditional independence of yield residuals.

Chapter 5 tests empirically three simple versions of a multi-index model and compares the findings to those reported for the single-index model in the previous two chapters.

Chapter 6 specifies the model to be used in this study, presents summary data for the mutual fund portfolios employed in the sample, and notes some of the limitations to be ascribed to the results.

Chapter 7 reports the results of applying the model to the sample of mutual-fund portfolios specifically with regard to the utility of the model as a deter-minant of one aspect of portfolio performance and also with regard to the issue of stationarity of portfolio volatility. It also offers suggestions for future research in this area.

Principal Findings

1. The systematic portion of individual security risk is not completely stationary, especially over the more recent time periods tested. And, the use of

---

[3]William F. Sharpe, "A Simplified Model for Portfolio Analysis," *Management Science* IX, no. 2 (January 1963): 277–293.

historical data to estimate security systematic risk leads to results that are not particularly sensitive to differencing interval within the same time horizon.

2. Residuals remaining after application of the market model to individual securities are not independent across securities but show a definite and broad correlation along industry lines.

3. A rather naive version of a multi-index model, employing industry indexes, is able to substantially reduce this correlation among residuals.

4. The proposed model for measuring portfolio risk exposure classifies mutual-fund portfolios in a manner substantially consistent with their stated investment objectives.

5. Portfolio systematic risk is not stationary for managed portfolios and investment companies appear to "manage" their portfolios to very different degrees.

6. Most portfolio managers rely on adjusting the fraction of the portfolio invested in cash to effect shifts in overall portfolio volatility.

7. Portfolio managers are not good predictors of market movements, as evidenced by shifts in portfolio volatility.

2

Portfolio Theory —
Risk Measurement —
Performance Criteria

Even in the world of the theoretician, armed with an arsenal of "simplifying assumptions," the decisions involved in solution of the portfolio problem are most complex. A typical definition of this problem as viewed by the theoretician follows.

We shall say that we have a portfolio problem if:
1. A finite number of investments are available.
2. The available capital can be divided up in any way among the investments.
3. All investments must be held for a certain period of time at the end of which they must be sold, or might as well be sold because the transaction cost of sale and repurchase is negligible.
4. The return per dollar on the ith investment does not depend on the amount invested in the ith or any other investment.
5. Preference is a function only of return on capital over the period of time in question.

. . .

The decision maker must choose the fraction of available capital to be invested in each investment.[1]

The solutions to the problem stated in this fashion are quite complicated even though they deal only with the "weighting" decision and to some extent rather superficially with the "selection" decision. Add to this the real-world problems of timing buy and sell decisions; the related problems of screening the great number of possible investments in order to arrive at a finite set of workable size; and the effort that must be exerted to collect and process the information required to formulate expectations about each security within this limited finite set. Consider also the problems occasioned by the nonperfect markets that make up the portfolio manager's operating environment. Information costs money; it is available neither universally nor simultaneously and it can be inaccurate or at least ambiguous. Contrary to Item 4 in the problem definition above, liquidity can frequently be a problem; and Item 3 above notwithstanding, there *are* transaction costs and taxes to be considered.

And finally, although they are not as readily identifiable, another set of problems faces the portfolio manager. The pressures to perform well in order to

---

[1] John W. Pratt, Howard Raiffa, and Robert Schlaifer, *Introduction to Statistical Decision Theory* (New York: McGraw Hill, 1965), p. 103.

compete with other managers for "that fraction of the savers' dollar" or the opportunity to manage a particular pension fund portfolio or just to equal last year's performance, themselves interact with and influence all of the other factors in this complex process.

How then, with a simple model, can we presume to measure the performance of a manager involved in making daily decisions within this terribly intricate process? We can't. However, we *can* isolate some of the factors that make up the investment process, set standards for these, and compare actual performance with these standards. Admittedly, there are facets of this problem that cannot be tested in this manner.

For example, we might consider a performance-measuring system concerned with:

A. The portfolio manager's ability to maintain a portfolio consistent with a stated investment objective with respect to:
    1. risk level
    2. income characteristics
    3. liquidity
B. The portfolio manager's ability to perform successfully.[2] This might consist of standards designed to measure his ability:
    1. to minimize risk through diversification
    2. to predict and take advantage of general market turns
    3. to buy undervalued and sell overvalued securities
    4. to correctly weight and time purchase and sale decisions
    5. to accomplish all of the above within established cost constraints

We believe that within limits, the development of existing theory regarding portfolio structure and the pricing of capital assets can be useful in developing and implementing such a performance-measuring system. In the context of the system described, this study is primarily concerned with Items A1, "the managers ability to maintain the desired risk level," and B2, "his ability to predict general market turns and to adjust his portfolio accordingly."

Portfolio Theory

It is almost axiomatic that any discussion of the literature of portfolio management begin with Markowitz.[3] In this case it is not superfluous, since the development of the theory of measuring portfolio performance closely parallels

---

[2] Perform in the general sense of the word as opposed to "performance investing."
[3] Harry M. Markowitz, "Portfolio Selection," *Journal of Finance* VII (March 1952): 77–91.

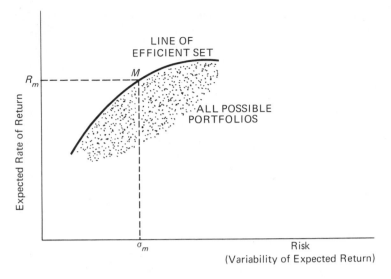

Figure 2-1. The Efficient Set.

the growth of knowledge in the area of portfolio selection. Markowitz—under some relatively strict assumptions about time horizons or holding periods, and the nature of the investor's preference function or the nature of the probability distributions of security returns—gave us the concept of an "efficient set." That is, if risk is measured by variance (variability of expected return) and if covariance among security returns is accounted for, the efficient set of portfolios is comprised of those combinations of securities where, for a given amount of risk, there is no other portfolio that provides a higher expected return and, conversely, for a given expected return there is no portfolio that carries less risk.

Diagrammatically the efficient set is shown in Figure 2-1, in which no other portfolio at risk level σ_m provides a higher expected return than R_m; portfolio M is efficient.

Markowitz went on to develop the mathematics to solve the parametric quadratic programming problem involved in computing the efficient set[4] and in 1958 expanded and added to the theory, presented in his original work, in a book entitled *Portfolio Selection: Efficient Diversification of Investments.* The book is important to the development of much of the application of the theory of portfolio selection, as well as to the development of means of measuring investment performance, solely because of a footnote that appears on page 100. This will be referred to later.

---

[4] Harry M. Markowitz, "The Optimization of a Quadratic Function Subject to Linear Constraints," *Naval Research Logistics Quarterly* III (1956): 111-133.

No significant contributions were made to the theory of portfolio selection between 1952 and 1958 by other writers in the field. In 1958 James Tobin applied the Markowitz notion of diversification in presenting a theory of liquidity preference.[5] At the same time, he provided an explicit definition of the types of utility functions implicit in the Markowitz-type portfolio analysis. And finally, he presented what is now known as the separation theorem. Basically this theorem states that the decision regarding the selection of an optimal portfolio and the decision regarding the degree of risk an investor is willing to bear are separate decisions for all investors. An investor can select the portfolio on the forefront of the efficient set, regardless of the inherent risk level and then adjust the risk level to suit his own tastes by borrowing or lending a riskless asset at a riskless rate, e.g., short-term government securities held to maturity or a savings bank account. This is expressed diagrammatically in Figure 2-2, where R^* is the rate of return on a riskless asset. Thus, for example, if an investor invests in portfolio M, he expects to earn a rate of return R_m. However, if M with its associated risk σ_m is too risky for his tastes, he can invest only a portion of his funds in M and invest (lend) the balance at rate R^*. This will reduce his risk level to σ_j and his expected rate of return to R_j. Conversely, if M is too conservative for him, he can invest all of his funds in M, borrow at a rate R^*, and invest the borrowings in M as well; thus levering up his position in order to earn the higher expected return R_k but bearing the greater risk σ_k. The trade-offs between risk and return (preference function) any investor is willing to make can also be portrayed on this diagram, and the optimal portfolio for the investor can be shown to be the point of tangency between the line $R^* - T$ and the investors particular preference function.

Rather than lose the logical development of the theory of measurement of portfolio performance let us move out of chronological sequence and jump to the work of John Lintner.[6]

Lintner, in his excellent work, clearly states and proves the separation theorem. In so doing he defines the angle Θ as shown in Figure 2-3. The reader will note that this is almost identical to Figure 2-2.

Θ is the slope of the $R^* - T$ line. It can also be stated as

$$\Theta_j = \frac{R_j - R^*}{\sigma_j}$$

i.e., the return in excess of the riskless rate per unit of risk. Note that this excess return is the premium for bearing risk. If an investor invested all of his money in

[5] James Tobin, "Liquidity Preference as Behavior Toward Risk" *Review of Economic Studies* XXV (February 1958): 65–86.
[6] John Lintner, "The Valuation of Risk Assets and the Selection of Risky Investments in Stock Portfolios and Capital Budgets." *Review of Economics and Statistics* LXVII (February 1965): 13–37; and "Security Prices, Risk and Maximal Gains from Diversification," *Journal of Finance* XX, no. 4 (December 1965): 587–615.

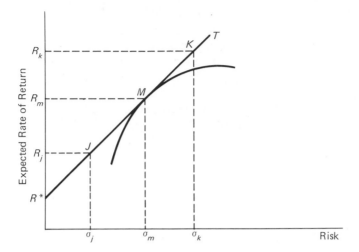

Figure 2-2. The Separation Theorem.

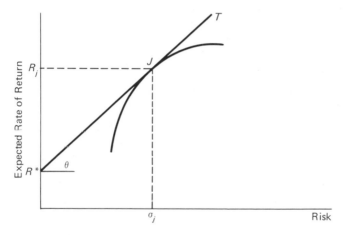

Figure 2-3. The Slope of the $R*$ - T Line.

the riskless asset he would receive the rate of return $R*$ and bear no risk. In order to earn a rate of return in excess of $R*$ he must bear some risk. But as Lintner points out and as is apparent from Figure 2-3, as Θ increases, i.e., as the slope of the line $R*$ - T increases, the excess rate of return per unit of risk increases; and thus *the best possible portfolio is the one which has the highest* Θ. Note.that as long as the investor is risk averse this holds regardless of the shape of his utility function. *This is the first step in the development of portfolio theory that directly implies a measure of performance.*

And, in fact, Sharpe does use Θ as a measure of performance.[7] Although Lintner dealt with expected return and risk, Sharpe utilizes Θ as a measure of return by treating risk and return in an ex-post sense. In this sense the excess return over the riskless rate is the "reward provided the investor for bearing risk" and the standard deviation of return shows the amount of risk actually borne. Sharpe very simply measured the annual rate of return for each of 34 mutual funds over a ten-year priod. He then computed the average rate of return for each fund and the standard deviation from this average. Then, using 3 percent as the riskless rate of return, he computed a Θ, of sorts, for each fund where

$$\Theta = \frac{\overline{R} - 3\%}{S}$$

$\overline{R}$ = average of 10 annual returns for each fund
S = standard deviation from this average

The main weakness of this procedure revolves around the use of a measure of risk that is presumed to remain unchanged over the ten-year period.

Annual rates of return also tend to obscure a good deal of the portfolio activity that occurs during the year; quarterly returns are more appropriate to a sensitive measure of portfolio performance. In addition, this is a gross measure of performance; it cannot answer any of the specific questions about investment performance posed at the outset of this chapter. And further, there is, of course, also the problem of using ex-post data in the context of an expectations model.

In spite of these shortcomings, Sharpe has brought the developments of Markowitz, Tobin, and Lintner from the realm of theory to practical application, and developed a reasonably good risk-adjusted performance measure.

Backtracking to 1958, let us pick up the Markowitz footnote and follow the parallel development of another line of thought which has direct bearing on the problem of evaluating investment performance.[8]

The application of Markowitz' theory to determine the efficient set was all but impossible because of the great number of assessments involved. A portfolio of 100 securities would require 5150 separate assessments of expected return, variance, and covariance, really an impossible task. The Markowitz footnote suggested that if the portfolio manager were willing to make the additional assumptions that security returns were jointly normal and related only through a common normally distributed market factor, the assessment problem would be considerably reduced. This is readily shown if we consider the relationship that such assumptions would create between two securities i and j.

---

[7]William F. Sharpe, "Mutual Fund Performance," *Journal of Business* XXXIX, no. 1, pt. II (January 1966): 119–138.

[8]Harry M. Markowitz, *Portfolio Selection,* 1958, p. 100 n.

$$\tilde{R}_i = a_i + b_i \tilde{M} + \tilde{e}_i \qquad \tilde{R}_j = a_j + b_j \tilde{M} + \tilde{e}_j$$

where M is the market factor, a_i and b_i are parameters of the ith security, and e_i is a normally distributed random element. It is further assumed that

$$E(\tilde{e}_i) = E(\tilde{e}_j) = 0 \qquad \text{cov } (\tilde{e}_i \tilde{M}) = \text{cov } (\tilde{e}_j \tilde{M}) = 0$$

then

$$
\begin{aligned}
\text{cov}(\tilde{R}_i \tilde{R}_j) \quad &= \quad E[(\tilde{R}_i - \bar{R}_i)(\tilde{R}_j - \bar{R}_j)] \\
&= \quad E[(a_i + b_i \tilde{M} + \tilde{e}_i - a_i - b_i \bar{M})(a_j + b_j \tilde{M} + \tilde{e}_j - a_j - b_j \bar{M})] \\
&= \quad E\{[b_i(\tilde{M} - \bar{M}) + \tilde{e}_i]\,[b_j(\tilde{M} - \bar{M}) + \tilde{e}_j]\}
\end{aligned}
$$

Letting

$$(\tilde{M} - \bar{M}) = \tilde{m}$$

Then

$$
\begin{aligned}
\text{cov } (\ ) \quad &= \quad E(b_i b_j \tilde{m}^2 + b_j \tilde{m} \tilde{e}_i + b_i \tilde{m} \tilde{e}_j + \tilde{e}_i \tilde{e}_j) \\
&= \quad b_i b_j V(\tilde{M}) + b_j \text{ cov}(\tilde{e}_i \tilde{M}) + b_i \text{ cov}(\tilde{e}_j \tilde{M}) + \text{cov}(\tilde{e}_i \tilde{e}_j) \\
&= \quad b_i b_j V(\tilde{M}) + \text{cov}(\tilde{e}_i \tilde{e}_j)
\end{aligned}
$$

Where the factor $b_i b_j V(\tilde{M})$ represents the variability of the market return and the relationship between the return of each security and that of the market, and where cov$(\tilde{e}_i \tilde{e}_j)$ now expresses the relationship between securities i and j, to the extent that it is not accounted for by the market. It is this latter factor that Markowitz suggested be assumed equal to zero in order to reduce the assessment problem. If this is done, then

$$\text{cov}(\tilde{R}_i \tilde{R}_j) = b_i b_j V(\tilde{M})$$

and the number of assessments required to compute the covariance among 100 securities is reduced from 4950 to 101.

Since this model provides the basis for the research presented herein, it is important that we discuss it fully. The idea of relating security returns to market movements is not unrealistic. The price movements of individual securities are clearly not independent of the direction of the market. We have all observed the effect of a significant political or economic happening on the market. Security prices tend to react together nearly simultaneously and move in the same direction. This model captures that portion of the comovement of security prices which is conditional on the market. Other types of news affect the price movements of subgroups of securities. Among the most common would be news affecting a particular sector of the economy. Consider, for example, the effect of passage of Medicare legislation on the nursing-home business. We would expect prices of stocks within this group to move upward together. Other information could similarly affect the price movements of two or more securities. The model proposed explicitly excludes the price movements common to these subgroups. All common price movements among securities, other than those shared with the market, will not be accounted for when we accept the assumption that $\text{cov}(\tilde{e}_i\,\tilde{e}_j)$ equals zero. These, of course, could be included within the model, if we were able to identify groups of securities that move together and were able to capture their commonality in some type of summary measure or index. Such indexes could then be incorporated into the model as added explanatory variables.

Individual security price movements caused by information unique to a particular security, such as a quarterly earnings report or the development of a new product, are captured by the model in the residual term e_i. The parameter b_i is in effect a measure of the responsiveness of the ith security to changes in the market, i.e., the volatility of the ith security. This parameter is of primary concern and its measurement and use is the subject of a considerable portion of the balance of this research.

Sharpe was the first to propose serious consideration of this "single-index" or "market" model.[9] He used it to accomplish two things (1) to greatly reduce the total number of assessments required to achieve a diversified portfolio, e.g., in the one hundred-security portfolio instance from 5150 to 302 and (2) by employing an analogue, which resulted in a diagonal covariance matrix, to significantly reduce the amount of computer time required to compute the efficient set. The latter contribution is not as significant now, given the speed of the current generation of computers. It might be noted though, that many computer packages designed to generate an efficient set do employ the Markowitz–Sharpe assumptions regarding the linear relationship of security returns with a market factor. Again, we are not concerned with this development as it pertains to portfolio selection but as it pertains to measuring investment performance. The idea of relating security returns to market returns in this manner, together with the use of the separation theorem, led to the nearly simultaneous development of capital-asset pricing models by Lintner, Sharpe, and Treynor.[10]

---

[9]William F. Sharpe, "A Simplified Model for Portfolio Analysis," *Management Science* IX, no. 2 (January 1963): 277–293.

[10]John Lintner, "The Valuation of Risk Assets and the Selection of Risky Investments in Stock Portfolios and Capital Budgets," *Review of Economics and Statistics* LXVII

Risk Measurement

The models of these researchers specify that, in equilibrium, the expected return on a security or portfolio of securities is a linear function of the co-variance of its return with that of the market portfolio. Thus, letting

$\tilde{R}_j$ = the return on the jth security

R^* = the rate of return on a riskless asset

$\tilde{R}_m$ = the return on the market portfolio

then

$$E(\tilde{R}_j) = R^* + \frac{E(\tilde{R}_m) - R^*}{\sigma^2(\tilde{R}_m)} \; \text{cov}(\tilde{R}_j\tilde{R}_m) \qquad (2.1)$$

Thus, the expected return on a risky asset or on a portfolio of risky assets is equal to the return that may be realized by investing in a riskless asset plus an additional return for bearing risk, where the term $[E(\tilde{R}_m) - R^*]/\sigma^2(\tilde{R}_m)$ is the market price per unit of risk and $\text{cov}(\tilde{R}_j\tilde{R}_m)$ is the measure of risk associated with the jth security or portfolio.

By defining

$$\beta_j = \frac{\text{cov}(\tilde{R}_j\tilde{R}_m)}{\sigma^2(\tilde{R}_m)}$$

equation (2.1) may be rewritten as

$$E(R_j) = R^* + [E(R_m) - R^*] \, \beta_j$$

The term β_j is often referred to as the systematic risk of the jth security, and represents the extent to which the return on asset j is dependent on the returns of the other securities in the market. The balance of the risk associated with the jth security is unique to that security and is not priced by the market, since the combination of securities in efficient portfolios eliminates this residual element of risk.

Fama, in an excellent treatment of the subject, has shown that β_j in the capital-asset model can be realistically approximated by the b_j of Sharpe's

(February 1965): 13–37; William F. Sharpe, "Capital Asset Prices: A Theory of Market Equilibrium Under Conditions of Risk," *Journal of Finance* XIX (September 1964): 425–442; and Jack L. Treynor, unpublished report.

single-index model, thus paving the way for the practical employment of the
capital asset pricing model.[11]

The importance of this model for our purposes is that it distinguishes between the two types of risk that can be measured within the context of the model. Total risk is said to be made up of *systematic risk* and *residual risk,* where systematic risk is that risk associated with the economy or the stock market in general. As long as one holds risky securities this risk will be present. Residual risk, on the other hand, is that risk not accounted for by the market, but is peculiar to an individual security. Residual risk can be eliminated through diversification; but systematic risk, since it is common to all securities, cannot be eliminated by any strategy involving the combination of risky securities.

The first attempt to apply this type of model to the problem of computing a risk-adjusted performance measure was made by Treynor.[12] Treynor proposed that the proper measure of portfolio performance is the slope of the "portfolio possibility line," which is shown in Figure 2–4. Each portfolio of course would have its own line in such a diagram.

The measure of risk proposed by Treynor is fund volatility, which is in fact the b_j of the Sharpe single-index model and Fama's proxy for systematic risk.[13] Note the similarities between Lintner's Θ and Treynor's slope of the "portfolio-possibility" line.

$$\Theta = \frac{\bar{R}_j - R^*}{\sigma_j} \qquad \text{Treynor slope} = \frac{\bar{R}_j - R^*}{b_j}$$

In the former case, standard deviation of returns (total risk) is used as a measure of risk. In the latter case, only the systematic portion of the risk element is used.

Treynor explicitly states the critical assumption that a fund's returns must be clustered around the "characteristic line" (single-index model regression line) for his measure to be meaningful. In terms of our previous discussion, Treynor assumes a good fit on the regression line or a small standard error of estimate. Since the standard error is a measure of the portfolio variance not explained by the market factor—i.e., a measure of residual risk—Treynor's assumption is that the residual risk is small and consequently *that the fund is efficiently diversified.* If the fund is not efficiently diversified, it is bearing some residual risk for which its holders may not be compensated and which Treynor's measure cannot detect. Some would argue that this is not really a defect in Treynor's measure, since if we are talking about a mutual-fund portfolio, it itself is probably just one of

---

[11] Eugene F. Fama, "Risk, Return and Equilibrium: Some Clarifying Comments," *Journal of Finance* XXIII, no. 1 (March 1968): 29–40.

[12] Jack L. Treynor, "How to Rate Management of Investment Funds," *Harvard Business Review* XLIII (January–February 1965): 63–75.

[13] Anachronism tolerated for sake of clarity. Treynor's work was published in 1965; Fama's in 1969.

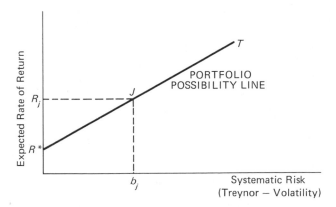

Figure 2–4. The Portfolio Possibility Line.

many assets that are held by an investor. To the extent that he still has the opportunity to diversify his *overall* portfolio, the investor will not be concerned with this risk and should aim for maximum expected return per unit of systematic risk regardless of the residual element. While this is true, we believe that a distinction can be made between external performance measures and internal performance measures. To the extent that diversification is a desirable goal, if we are to measure a portfolio manager's ability either objectively or within an organization relative to other portfolio managers, ability to diversify should be one criterion of performance and total risk as well as systematic risk should be a standard.

State of the Art

At this point the excellent work of Michael C. Jensen is of particular interest because it incorporates most of the theory and research findings published to date.[14] Also, the research reported herein is the next logical step in the development of a system for measuring the performance of portfolio managers and builds on the work of Jensen.

Basically, Jensen used the capital-asset pricing model developed by Sharpe and Lintner to evaluate a portfolio manager's performance. Jensen's work centered on determining whether the returns on a sample of 115 mutual funds were consistent with their level of systematic risk. For each of his sample

[14] Michael C. Jensen, "The Performance of Mutual Funds in the Period 1945–1964," *Journal of Finance* XXIII no. 2 (May 1968): 389–419; and "Risk the Pricing of Capital Assets, and the Evaluation of Investment Portfolios," *Journal of Business* LXII, no. 2 (April 1969): 167–247.

funds Jensen computes b_j, using regression techniques based on ten to twenty
years of logarithmically transformed annual wealth relatives for the funds and for
the Standard & Poor Composite 500 Price Index. Two critical assumptions underlying the model are that portfolio b_j's are stationary over time and that they are
invariant to the length of the time interval over which returns are measured.
Jensen tests these assumptions for the 56 funds for which 20 years of data are
available, with mixed results. The test for invariance to the length of the differencing interval over which returns are calculated involves the computation of
b_j based on both one-year and two-year rates of return over the same twenty-
year period. The correlation between the two sets of b_j is 0.89, suggesting that
this is not a bad assumption.

The test for stationarity involves computing the regression coefficient b_j for
each of the two consecutive ten-year periods and computing the correlation
between the respective b_js. The correlation between the two estimates is 0.74.
While this may be high enough (when dealing with funds in general) to proceed
under the assumption that b_js are approximately stationary over successive ten-
year intervals, the differences in individual-fund systematic-risk elements over
time can be large. For example, Jensen's data show a range of *differences* in b_j
from one ten-year period to the next of -0.764 to +0.146. If the two extreme
outliers are not considered, this interval remains a fairly sizeable -0.469 to
+0.133. Since this element of systematic risk is critical in assessing the performance of individual portfolio managers, these differences are significant; they
are certainly large enough to cause an evaluator of portfolio performance to be
uncomfortable with the stationarity assumption.

Perhaps even more important, since the values of b_j computed for the fund
portfolios are, in fact, averages for each of the ten-year periods, there might still
be substantial *within-period* variance about these averages; but this is not taken
into account.

Treynor has also done some work involving tests of stationarity.[15] He has
examined annual returns for 54 funds and attempted to fit a quadratic function
to the data, i.e., a function with a changing slope, b, vs. the constant slope of
the linear regression function. He concluded, on the basis of the standard F test
that no curvature exists. This is a good test, if funds did outguess the market
we would expect their portfolios to consist of more volatile securities (higher b)
when the fund manager anticipated a market upswing and less volatile securities
(lower b) when a downswing was forecast. Unfortunately, Treynor's work has
two shortcomings: (1) only a quadratic function was used to test curvature, and
more importantly (2) only ten rates of return were used and these were annual
data. Although not as readily available at that time, quarterly data would have

---

[15] Jack L. Treynor and Kay K. Mazuy, "Can Mutual Funds Outguess the Market,"
Harvard Business Review XLIV (July, August 1966): 131-136.

been more appropriate. In most years, the market moves in more than one direction during the year. In 1968, for example, in judging whether a portfolio manager was able to adjust portfolio volatility prior to market swings, the criteria most certainly would not be opening and closing net asset values and dividend distributions, as implied by Treynor's work.

Jensen does not test the basic assumption of the market model that security returns are related only through the market factor, i.e., $\operatorname{cov}(\tilde{e}_i\, \tilde{e}_j)$ is zero for $i \neq j$.

Jensen's work is primarily concerned with portfolio managers' ability to identify and deal in undervalued and overvalued securities, thereby earning returns greater than those expected given the portfolios' levels of systematic risk. His model is of little use in appraising other aspects of portfolio management, such as the manager's ability to maintain a risk level consistent with the portfolio's objective or his ability to adjust portfolio composition correctly in anticipation of changes in the capital markets. For example, a systematic risk factor b_j of 1.20 might be computed for the Dreyfus Fund for the period 1958–1968; i.e., over this ten-year interval, the Dreyfus Fund, on the average, was 1.2 times as risky as the market as a whole. If the market moved 10 percent in either direction, the Dreyfus portfolio would typically move 12 percent in the same direction. If it were part of Dreyfus' objective to maintain a portfolio that could potentially absorb a risk 1.2 times as great as the general market risk, *on the average* the portfolio manager successfully accomplished this goal over this particular ten-year interval. No statement can be made about his performance for the last quarter or even the last year, or two years.

Systematic risk, then, computed in this manner is not responsive to short-term changes in portfolio composition, changes which are the essence of a "managed" portfolio. It does not provide the manager himself with guidelines for action, nor can it be used to assess his performance for time intervals of less than ten years. The research described herein treats this problem.

Given the market model as previously described, relating the returns of the jth security to those in the market,

$$\tilde{R}_j = a_j + b_j \tilde{R}_m + \tilde{e}_j$$

Recall that b_j is a measure of the responsiveness of the jth security to changes in the market. If we not consider a portfolio of n securities where X_{jt} is the fraction of the portfolio invested in the jth security at time t then

$$\sum_{j=1}^{n} X_{jt} = 1$$

and the expected return of the portfolio at time t is the weighted sum of the
expected returns of the n securities at time t

$$E(\widetilde{R}_{pt}) = \sum_{j=1}^{n} X_{jt}E(\widetilde{R}_{jt})$$

Similarly the responsiveness of the portfolio's return to the return of the market
is the weighted sum of the volatilities of the assets making up the portfolio, viz.

$$B_t = \sum_{j=1}^{n} X_{jt}b_j$$

Using this result *we can measure portfolio volatility for any portfolio at any
given time.*

In computing b_j for individual securities, however, there exist the same
problems faced by Jensen on the portfolio level—stationarity, invariance to
differencing intervals, and independence conditional on market returns.

Chapter 3 reports the results of empirical tests conducted to determine the
effect that these factors might have on the proposed model. In addition, we also
tested the assumption of conditional independence of security returns, given
market returns, i.e., that $\text{cov}(\widetilde{e}_i \widetilde{e}_j) = 0$. The results of these tests are presented
in Chapter 4.

3 The Market Model — Individual Securities

Since the values determined for the coefficients of individual security b are critical to the proposed study of portfolio volatility, it is essential that we determine the sensitivity of these values to various assumptions that may be employed in their computation. The first phase of the research will therefore be concerned with the comovement of individual security prices with the market, where the market is represented by some broadly based index. Individual security b_i's will be computed within the framework of the single-index market model.

Recalling the market model presented in Chapter 2 we have

$$\widetilde{R}_{it} = a_{it} + b_{it}\widetilde{R}_{mt} + \widetilde{e}_{it}$$

If we assume that the distribution of changes in the logarithms of security prices is normal and further define

P_{it} = the price of security i at time t

$\widetilde{P}_{i(t+\tau)}$ = the price of security i, adjusted for dividends and distributions at time $t + \tau$

τ = a time interval, e.g., month, quarter, year

M_t = the level of the Standard & Poor's Composite 500 Stock Index at time t

$\widetilde{M}_{(t+\tau)}$ = the level of the Standard & Poor's Composite 500 Stock Index, adjusted for distributions at time $t + \tau$

then

$$\widetilde{R} = \log\frac{\widetilde{P}_{i(t+\tau)}}{P_{it}} \qquad \widetilde{R}_{mt} = \log\frac{\widetilde{M}_{t+\tau}}{M_t}$$

The parameters a_{it} and b_{it} are specific to the ith security. The subscript t refers

19

to a more general case where these characteristics are allowed to change over time. We define $\tilde{e}_{it}$ as a residual normally distributed with expectation of 0.

$$\left.\begin{array}{l} \text{cov}(\tilde{e}_{it}\tilde{R}_{mt}) \\ \\ \text{cov}(\tilde{e}_{it}\,\tilde{e}_{jt}) \end{array}\right\} = 0 \text{ for } i \neq j$$

Our primary interests at this point lie in determining and examining the b_{it} coefficients generated by the model for a wide range of securities, with particular concern for considerations of horizon time, differencing interval, and stationarity. Chapter 4 will describe additional tests made to examine the assumption of independence of individual security returns conditional on market returns.

"Horizon time" refers to the length of the time period over which the values of individual security b's are computed. "Differencing interval" deals with the frequency of observation of security returns. Do computed values of b_{it} vary with the length of the time period considered, e.g., five years vs. ten years; or are the values of b_{it} sensitive to the interval τ over which security returns are calculated, e.g., monthly vs. quarterly returns? "Stationarity" refers to the stability over time of b values computed for a given security. Would b_{it}, computed for the time interval $t = 1951 - 1960$, be a good estimate of the appropriate b_{it} for time interval $t = 1961 - 1970$?

With respect to the balance of the relationship described by the model, although it is not critical to the use of the model, it will be of interest to note the values assumed by a_{it}, as well as to determine the extent to which the model is able to explain the variance of individual security price changes.

The model was used to determine a_{it} and b_{it} values for samples of New York Stock Exchange securities. The samples were made up of all the securities listed continuously on the NYSE during the test periods. The basic security data were obtained from the price relative tape of the University of Chicago Center for Research in Security Prices. The variable "PR 1," a monthly security price relative—adjusted for all dividends and stock splits—was used to determine the dependent variable for each security. As noted, the index used as the independent variable was the Standard & Poor's Composite 500 stock index.[1] Dividend data for the S&P 500 are available only in the form of twelve-month moving totals, updated quarterly. These were converted to proportional monthly and quarterly figures where required.

We would expect that if the S&P 500 index is a fair representation of the market and if the sample is unbiased, the mean beta would be near 1.0, while the mean intercept, alpha, would be close to 0. It is unlikely that the mean beta

---

[1] Standard & Poor's Corporation, *Standard & Poor's Trade and Securities Statistics: Security Price Index Record* (Orange, Conn.: Standard & Poor's Corporation, 1968).

will be exactly 1.0, since the S&P 500 index is not composed of the same securities that make up the sample and also because the index is a *weighted* average of the 500 securities (the weights being the number of shares outstanding). To the extent that the S&P 500 tends to represent a relatively more conservative (stable) element of the Exchange, it can be expected that an unweighted average of b's for a sample of securities, somewhat arbitrarily chosen, will be greater than 1.0.[2]

The results of tests of the model for thirteen time periods are shown in Table 3-1. The full distribution of security betas and R^2's are shown for the interval 1956-1966 in Figure 3-1 and for other recent time periods in the Appendix.

General Findings

The results reported are consistent with what might reasonably be expected. In all instances, mean alphas are 0 or very close to it and not statistically significant. Mean betas are near 1.0 and highly significant (only where the 5-year time interval was employed are the t values less than 3 standard deviations from 0.[3] The movement of the mean beta from 1.24 in the two early decades to 1.13 and 1.05 in the two latter decades probably reflects the composition of the Standard & Poor's Index. Prior to 1941, the S&P composite index is linked to Cowles index, while from 1941-1954 the S&P index contained only 90 securities. Only since 1958 has it reflected the degree of market breadth provided by the inclusion of 500 securities. As already noted, to the extent that the index represents the more stable securities in the market, we can expect the mean value of beta for all securities to be greater than 1.0.

The mean values of the coefficients of determination for the individual securities, mean R^2, deserve separate comment, in light of the fact that they may appear inconsistent with what is generally accepted as "King's results." King, using factor analysis, examined comovement with the market of changes in log price for 63 securities over the period June 1927 through December 1960.[4] For this overall period, King concluded that "the typical stock has about half [52 percent] of its variance explained by an element of price change that affects the whole market." It is this result that is most referred to in King's work and which appears to contradict the values of R^2 reported here.

---

[2] The sample for each time period consists of all the securities continuously listed on the New York Stock Exchange during that period.

[3] The terms beta and b_j are used interchangeably in the text.

[4] Benjamin F. King, "Market and Industry Factors in Stock Price Behavior," *Journal of Business* XXXIX, no. 1, pt. II (January 1966): 139-190.

Table 3-1
Summary Statistics: Market Model – NYSE Securities

Time Period	Code	Observation Interval[a]	N[b]	Mean Alpha[c]	Mean Beta[c]	Mean R^2	Median Beta	Beta Range Low–High
1926–1946	20A	Q	216	-0.007 (0.17)	1.133 (8.43)	0.456	1.160	0.107–2.225
1946–1966	20B	Q	569	-0.007 (0.43)	1.077 (6.39)	0.331	1.058	0.122–2.210
1926–1936	10A	Q	315	-0.020 (0.45)	1.235 (5.79)	0.443	1.255	-0.133–2.658
1936–1946	10B	Q	549	0.000 (0.14)	1.237 (6.33)	0.492	1.214	0.292–2.525
1946–1956	10C	Q	569	-0.016 (0.75)	1.132 (4.80)	0.366	1.106	0.054–2.732
1956–1966	10D	Q	569	-0.001 (0.04)	1.051 (4.55)	0.333	1.024	-0.230–2.409
1946–1951	5(1)	Q	569	-0.014 (0.49)	1.264 (4.11)	0.454	1.229	0.225–3.330
1951–1956	5(2)	Q	569	-0.011 (0.29)	0.950 (2.57)	0.269	0.919	-0.558–3.187
1956–1961	5(3)	Q	569	-0.001 (0.09)	0.986 (2.86)	0.306	0.968	-0.208–2.872
1961–1966	5(4)	Q	569	-0.001 (0.04)	1.097 (3.83)	0.401	1.043	-0.608–3.545
1946–1966	20B	M	569	-0.002 (0.29)	1.002 (9.62)	0.273		
1956–1966	10D	M	569	0.000 (0.10)	0.999 (6.32)	0.245		
1961–1966	5(4)	M	569	0.000 (0.04)	1.112 (5.01)	0.281		

[a] Q = quarterly and M = monthly.
[b] N = number of securities for which statistics were computed.
[c] t values are shown in parentheses.

Mean Regression Statistics for 569 Securities

Alpha	–0.001	Beta	1.051	R^2	0.333
t	(–0.037)		(4.553)		

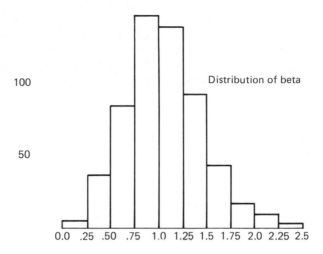

Distribution of beta

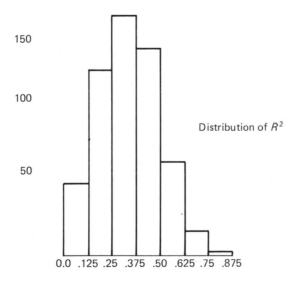

Distribution of R^2

Figure 3-1. Distribution of Security Beta and R^2 Values: Quarterly Observations – January 1956 to June 1966.

But note that King also found considerable variation in R^2 for various time intervals. For he also states:

This time behavior of the market component of variance is reflected in the *downward drift* in the subperiod means. Whereas approximately 58 percent of the variance, on the average, was attributable to the market from June, 1927, through September, 1935, *the average proportion of variance due to the market is only about 31 percent during the last subperiod.* In other words, the influence of a general comovement effect on the stock market seems to have diminished over the years.[5]

Note that the mean R^2 in Table 3-1 decreases from a high of 0.492 in the two early decades to 0.366 and 0.333 in the next ten-year periods. This appears entirely consistent with King's findings.

Differencing Intervals and Length of Time Period

One objective of this analysis was to determine the effect on the values of individual security betas of using different observation intervals and different time periods. Since we will ultimately be concerned with relatively current portfolios, testing was limited to the 1946-1966 period. Within this period, the model was employed using both quarterly and monthly observations for these subperiods. For convenience the pertinent data have been extracted from Table 3-1 and appear as Table 3-2.

Note that the values of beta based on quarterly observations are highly correlated with those based on monthly observations. Note also that the values of mean R^2 are consistently lower when monthly observations are substituted for quarterly observations in the model. This can perhaps be attributed to an increase in random noise elements associated with observations based on the shorter differencing interval, in effect new information unique to a particular security is a more significant factor in the short run.

A second and related objective was to determine the sensitivity of beta to the length of the time interval used to observe security price movements. That is, should we use twenty years of data or ten or even five in computing beta? Using the same three time intervals as above, we arbitrarily selected the betas computed for the period 1956-1966 (quarterly observations) as a standard and correlated with this standard the betas computed for the remaining "time period/observation frequency" combinations. The resulting correlation coefficients are shown in Table 3-3.

Correlation coefficients are high. Security *b* values based on both five- and

---

[5] Ibid. The last subperiod referred to was August 1952 through December 1960. The italics are mine.

Table 3-2
Model Results: NYSE Securities – Quarterly vs. Monthly Observations

Time Period	Quarterly Observations			Monthly Observations			Correlation of Security Betas (Monthly vs. Quarterly)
	Mean Alpha	Mean Beta	Mean R^2	Mean Alpha	Mean Beta	Mean R^2	
1946–1966	−0.007	1.077	0.331	−0.002	1.002	0.273	0.912
1956–1966	−0.001	1.051	0.333	0.000	0.999	0.245	0.883
1961–1966	−0.001	1.097	0.401	0.000	1.112	0.281	0.839

Table 3–3
Security Beta Correlations (569 Securities)

Time Period	Correlation with 1956–1966 Time Period	
	Quarterly Observations	Monthly Observations
1946–1966	0.871	0.765
1956–1966	1.000	0.883
1961–1966	0.829	0.785

twenty-year time horizons are highly correlated with similar values determined for a ten-year interval. Security betas do not appear particularly sensitive to the length of the time interval used, over the period tested.

Stationarity

A final test was designed to examine the stationarity of individual security betas. The forty-year period, 1926–1966, was divided into two twenty-year and four ten-year subperiods. Security betas, using quarterly observations, were computed for all of the securities which were on the CRSP tape continuously for each subperiod. These betas were then correlated for successive subperiods. Table 3–4 shows the resultant product moment and rank order correlation coefficients.

The correlations shown for both the twenty-year and ten-year periods over which values of b_{it} were compared, indicate some limited stationarity of security betas over time. The drop in the correlation coefficient from 0.708 to 0.507 for the most recent ten-year comparisons is, however, a rather strong indication that individual security b values may not be considered constant over these two decades. And again, since the values of b are averages for each time interval tested, we cannot comment on intraperiod stationarity.

However, Blume has suggested in a recent article that in the context of a large portfolio an investor *might be willing to act as if his assessments of a_i and b_i were certain.*

The reason is that if an investor's assessments of a_i and β_i were unbiased and the errors in these assessments were independent among the different assets, his uncertainty attached to his assessments of $\bar{a}$ and $\bar{\beta}$, merely weighted averages of the a_i's and β_i's, would tend to become smaller, the larger the number of assets in the portfolios and the smaller the proportion in each asset. Intuitively, the errors in the assessments of a_i and β_i would tend to offset each other.

This discussion suggests that the predictive distributions assessed under the

Table 3–4

Model Results: NYSE Securities – Tests of Stationarity of b_{it}

Time Period t		Time Period t – d	Interval	Correlation of b_{it} with b_i (t – d)	Rank Order Correlation of b_{it} with b_i (t – d)	Number of Securities
1946–1966	vs.	1926–1946	20 years	0.671	0.671	216
1936–1946	vs.	1926–1936	10 years	0.655	0.664	315
1946–1956	vs.	1936–1946	10 years	0.707	0.708	549
1956–1966	vs.	1946–1956	10 years	0.513	0.507	569

assumption that a_i and β_i are constants will better approximate the underlying distributions, the larger the number of securities in the portfolios.[6]

Therefore from the viewpoint of a portfolio manager, as opposed to an investor concerned with an investment in a single security, the fact that b_i is not absolutely stationary over time may well be of little concern. It is the composite portfolio risk posture that is critical. And it is this factor we shall examine in some detail in the later chapters.

Miscellaneous Findings

In light of the premium that Markowitz portfolio analysis places on securities with a negative covariance, it is interesting to note that the ranges of security beta values shown in Table 3-1 reflect the fact that some securities do indeed appear to be negatively correlated with the Standard & Poor's index. Interestingly enough, for the 1926-1936 decade as well as for the most recent five- and ten-year periods, the securities with negative values of b_{it} are all gold mining stocks. The particular securities and their b values are shown in Table 3-5.

It is particularly comforting, for those of us who are interested in the practical application of these "theoretical" models, that this particular model has unequivocally identified the very securities that market observers consider to move counter to the market.

Consider the following from a recent financial news column.

There's no doubt about it. Gold issues seem to make a habit of going one way when the general stock market is headed in a different direction.

Consider, for example, what happened last Wednesday.

The market scored its best gain in more than a year as the Dow-Jones Industrial Average boomed 16.08 points. Volume on the New York Stock Exchange, at the same time, soared to 19.35 million shares, by far the largest turnover of 1969.

It was undoubtedly a day when bullish forces held the fort on Wall Street.

But while the general list was climbing exuberantly, these representative gold stocks turned downward as follows:

*American–South African Investment, off $1\frac{1}{2}$ to $59\frac{3}{4}$
*Campbell Red Lake Mines off $1\frac{3}{8}$ to $35\frac{1}{8}$
*Homestake Mining, off $1\frac{3}{8}$ to $40\frac{1}{8}$
*Dome Mines, off $\frac{3}{8}$ to $73\frac{3}{4}$.

It would appear that gold stocks march to the beat of a different drummer.[7]

---

[6] Marshall Blume, "Portfolio Theory:: A Step Toward Its Practical Application," *Journal of Business* XLIII, no. 2 (April 1970): 152–173.

[7] Vartanig G. Vartan, "Gold Issues Show Trend in Reverse," Spotlight: *New York Times,* May 4, 1969.

Table 3-5
Securities with Negative Values of b_{it}

Period	Security	Values of b_{it}
1926–1936	Homestake Mining	−0.1332
1956–1966	Homestake Mining	−0.2297
	Campbell Red Lake Mines[a]	−0.2685
1961–1966	Homestake Mining	−0.5855
	Dome Mines Limited	−0.6077

[a]Not included in Table 3–1, since it was not listed on the NYSE for the full 1946–1966 period.

Summary

Security betas do not appear sensitive to the differencing interval used. The model was able to explain more of the variance in security price changes, however, when quarterly observations were employed. It also appears that values of b computed for various time horizons are not significantly affected by the length of the time interval considered.

The evidence is not as positive in the tests made for stationarity with this model. There is correlation among security b values computed for different time periods. However, correlation coefficients of the order 0.50 to 0.70 are sufficiently removed from 1.0 to make us uncomfortable with the stationarity assumption, particularly for the more recent time periods.

4

Testing the Market
Model — Residuals

Challengers of the market model, on both theoretical and pragmatic grounds, share a common misgiving. The theoretician questions the assumption that security price changes are conditionally independent given the market. Stated in another fashion, the theoreticians do not consider it safe to assume that individual security price changes are not related except to the extent that they share a common relationship with an overall market movement. The practitioner questions the validity of any model based solely on a *market* factor. His experience leads him to believe that securities move in groups. Industry groups are the prime example. It is certainly not unusual, for example, to observe airline stocks or computer stocks moving independently of the market. Other less formal classifications of common stocks have been developed over time, primarily in order to group securities that tend to move in unison. Thus, we have "blue chips," "growth stocks," "defensive stocks," "cyclical stocks," etc.

In the terminology of the foregoing model, we are talking about the assumption that $\text{cov}(\widetilde{e}_i\,\widetilde{e}_j) = 0$ for $i \neq j$. That is to say, that after removing the effect of the market, are the yield residuals $\widetilde{e}_i$ and $\widetilde{e}_j$ for all pairs of securities independent? Are they unique to the individual securities considered or do they share some further commonality? The purpose of this chapter is to report the nature and results of a test conducted to investigate this assumption.

The Test

The test itself is simple and straightforward. Select a sample of securities, run them through the market model, compute the residuals, and construct the correlation matrix showing the relationship among the residuals of all possible pairs of securities in the sample. Then test the structure of the resultant correlation matrix to determine if it could have been generated by independent residuals. Also observe the nature of the securities involved with the extreme maximum and minimum correlations in an effort to identify possible underlying systematic elements.

The potential sample was limited to the 569 New York Stock Exchange securities that are listed continuously on the CRSP[1] price-relative tape from

---

[1] University of Chicago Center for Research in Security Prices.

December 1945 through June 1966. Thus, 246 monthly observations were available for each security. A sample of 100 securities was selected from the 569 for
the test. In order to insure that the securities in the sample were representative
of mutual-fund investments over the past two decades, sixty-five of the one
hundred securities were selected from the lists of Vickers Favorite Fifty for the
years 1946, 1960, and 1969.[2] These 65 include all of the securities common to
the Vickers lists and the CRSP 569. The remaining 35 securities were drawn at
random from the balance of 503 securities available on the Chicago tape. In
order to insure some degree of breadth among industry classes within the sample
of 35 securities selected at random, the number of securities drawn from each
industry group was in direct proportion to that group's representation among the
569 original securities.[3] The securities used in the sample are listed in Table 4-1
by industry code. The source of each security is also noted.

For purposes of general comparison, Table 4-2 describes the industry
breakdown of the sample together with a similar breakdown for the 569 available securities.

Structure of the Correlation Matrix

A typical portion of the resultant 100×100 correlation matrix is shown in
Table 4-3. For the most part the correlations are small. The mean of the 4950
correlations is 0.0325. They range, however, from -0.3935 to 0.7382. Relatively
high correlations appear in the sample portion of the matrix, shown in Table 4-3,
with the 0.4591 correlation coefficient of security 31 with security 63 and in
the 0.4176 correlation between securities 60 and 62.

Of particular interest is the nature of the securities at the extremes of the
range of correlation coefficients in this matrix. The program that generated the
correlation matrix also saved and identified the particular pairs of securities
having the one hundred highest and one hundred lowest correlation coefficients.
Portions of both these one hundred pairings showing the correlation coefficients, the names and numbers of the securities, and their respective industries
are shown as Tables 4-4 and 4-5.

Of the one hundred paired securities at the *low* end of the range of
correlation coefficients, there are no instances when the two securities in
question have the same three-digit industry classification. Nor within pairs do
any of the securities belong to a common two-digit industry class. And there

---

[2] Vickers Favorite Fifty is a ranking by dollar value of the 50 listed common stocks
most widely held within investment-company portfolios (published quarterly by Vickers
Associates, Huntington, New York). The survey on which the list is based includes the
holdings of approximately 500 investment companies. The 1946 Favorite Fifty was compiled
by Wiesenberger & Co., New York, New York.

[3] In cases where more than one industry code was listed for a particular security, the
most recent was used.

Table 4–1
Sample of 100 Securities Used to Test Correlation of Error Terms

Security Code	Company	Industry	Source
744	HOMESTAKE MINING CO	104	R
40	AMERADA PETROLEUM CORP	131	V60
122	ARMOUR & CO	201	R
1169	PET MILK	202	R
1355	STANDARD BRANDS	204	V46
1497	UNITED BISCUIT CO OF AMER	205	R
1165	PEPSI COLA CO	209	R
1179	PHILIP MORRIS INC	211	V69
1242	REYNOLDS TOBACCO	211	R
721	HELME PRODUCTS INC	213	R
1316	SIMMONS CO	251	R
426	CROWN ZELLERBACH CORP	262	V69
793	INTERNATIONAL PAPER	262	V69
25	ALLIED CHEMICAL CORP	281	V60
286	CELANESE CORP OF AMERICA	281	V46
487	DOW CHEMICAL CO	281	V60
497	DUPONT	281	V69
1020	MONSANTO CO	281	V46
7	ABBOTT LABORATORIES	283	R
70	AMERICAN HOME PRODUCTS	283	V69
1143	PARKE DAVIS	283	V60
1200	PROCTOR & GAMBLE CO	284	V69
1057	NATIONAL LEAD CO	285	V60
1482	UNION CARBIDE CORP	287	V69
142	ATLAS CHEMICAL INDUSTRIES	289	R
724	HERCULES POWDER CO	289	V46
997	CONTINENTAL OIL	291	V69
998	GULF OIL CORP	291	V69
1181	PHILLIPS PETROLEUM	291	V69
1308	SHELL OIL CO	291	V60
1322	SKELLY OIL	291	R
1358	STANDARD OIL OF CALIF	291	V69
1359	STANDARD OIL OF INDIANA	291	V69
1361	STANDARD OIL OF NEW JERSEY	291	V69
1432	TEXACO	291	V69
572	FIRESTONE TIRE & RUBBER CO	301	V46
659	GOODRICH BF	301	V46
661	GOODYEAR TIRE AND RUBBER	301	V69
1536	US RUBBER	301	V46
532	ENDICOTT JOHNSON CORP	314	R
635	GENERAL REFRACTORIES CO	325	R
825	JOHNSMANVILLE	326	V46
1527	UNITED STATES GYPSUM	326	V60
21	ALLEGHENY LUDLUM STEEL	331	R
119	ARMCO STEEL CORP	331	V60
195	BETHLEHEM STEEL CORP	331	V60
831	JONES & LAUGHLIN STEEL CORP	331	R
1234	REPUBLIC STEEL CORP	331	V60
1305	SHARON STEEL CORP	331	R
1540	US STEEL	331	V60
303	CERRO CORP	333	R
790	INTERNATIONAL NICKEL	333	V69
848	KENNECOTT COPPER	333	V46

33

Table 4–1, cont.

Security Code	Company	Industry	Source
1176	PHELPS DODGE	333	V46
1239	REYNOLDS METALS	333	V60
52	AMERICAN CAN CO	341	R
395	CONTINENTAL CAN CO INC	341	V69
651	GILLETTE CO	342	V60
87	AMERICAN RADIATOR CO	343	V46
31	ALLIS CHALMERS MFG CO	352	R
282	CATERPILLAR TRACTOR CO	352	V69
451	DEERE & CO	352	V46
785	INTERNATIONAL HARVESTER	352	V46
1115	OTIS ELEVATOR	352	R
1452	TIMKEN ROLLER BEARING	356	R
249	BURROUGHS CORP	357	V69
782	IBM CORP	357	V69
46	AMERICAN BOSCH ARMA CORP	361	R
623	GENERAL ELECTRIC	361	V69
11	ADMIRAL CORPORATION	365	R
641	GENERAL TELEPHONE & ELEC	366	V60
806	INTERNATIONAL TEL & TEL	366	V69
1352	SPERRY RAND CORP	366	V69
333	CHRYSLER CORP	371	V69
510	EATON MANUFACTURING CO	371	R
629	GENERAL MOTORS	371	V69
1257	ROCKWELL STANDARD CORP	371	R
2	ACF INDUSTRIES INC	374	R
745	HONEYWELL INC	381	V69
508	EASTMAN KODAK	383	V69
123	ARMSTRONG CORK CO	398	V46
321	CHICAGO MILWAUKEE ST PAUL RR	401	R
1089	NORFOLK & WESTERN RY	401	R
683	GREYHOUND CORP	413	V46
1531	US LINES CO NJ	441	R
1099	NORTHWEST AIRLINES	451	V69
98	AT&T CO	481	V69
1157	PENNSYLVANIA POWER & LIGHT	491	R
1335	SOUTHERN CO	491	V60
380	CONSOLIDATED EDISON CO NY	492	R
28	ALLIED STORES CORP	531	V46
344	CITY STORES CO	531	R
1025	MONTGOMERY WARD	532	V46
1298	SEARS ROEBUCK	532	V69
863	KRESGE SS	533	V69
574	FIRST NATIONAL STORES INC	541	R
253	CIT FINANCIAL	614	V46
752	HOUSEHOLD FINANCE	614	V69
1008	MISSION CORP	671	R
1472	TWENTIETH CENTURY FOX FILM	781	R

R   = Security selected at random
V46 = Vickers Favorite Fifty 1946
V60 = Vickers Favorite Fifty 1960
V69 = Vickers Favorite Fifty 1969

34

Table 4–2
Sample of 100 Securities by Industry

Industry Code	Sample of 100		Available 569	
	Number	Percent of Total	Number	Percent of Total
0 – 99	0	0.0	2	0.3
100 – 199	2	2.0	19	3.3
200 – 299	33	33.0	158	27.8
300 – 399	46	46.0	226	39.9
400 – 499	9	9.0	79	13.8
500 – 599	6	6.0	47	8.3
600 – 699	3	3.0	32	5.6
700 – 799	1	1.0	6	1.0
Totals	100	100.0%	569	100.0%

are but sixteen instances, among these one hundred, where the paired securities carry the same one-digit classification. Conversely for the one hundred paired securities, exhibiting the *highest* correlation of residuals, there are just thirty cases where the securities within the pairs *are not* matched exactly *at the three-digit industry level.* And on closer examination, each of these thirty provides an interesting exception. For example, the highest correlation among residuals in the entire matrix, 0.7382, involves Skelly Oil and Mission Corporation, industry codes 291 and 671 respectively, a petroleum refining company and a holding company. However, as of December 31, 1966, Mission Corporation owned 71 percent of the common stock of Skelly Oil. If Mission Corporation therefore is considered to act as a petroleum refining company, the number of instances where pairs of securities do not have identical three-digit industry codes is reduced from thirty to twenty one.[4] Another exception is provided by Amerada Petroleum Corporation, carried with an industry code of 131. Amerada is involved six times in the one hundred highest correlations, in each instance with a petroleum refining company. Taking this into account, the number of paired three-digit industry codes that do not match is reduced to fifteen. Of these fifteen, the industry codes of four are matched at the two-digit level. The names and industry codes of the remaining eleven are detailed in Table 4-6.

The other relations brought out in Table 4-5 are also interesting. Residuals of U.S. Steel are highly correlated with those of Jones & Laughlin Steel, Republic Steel, Bethlehem Steel, and Armco Steel. The residuals of Goodyear Tire and Rubber appear on the list highly correlated with those of Firestone Tire and Rubber. Other notable pairings include International Paper wth Crown Zellerbach; Monsanto with Dow Chemical; Reynolds Tobacco with Phillip

---

[4] Market model residuals for Mission Corporation are also highly correlated with the residuals of eight other petroleum refining companies.

Table 4-3
A Typical Portion of the Correlation Matrix

Column	61	62	63	64	65	66	67	68	69	70
1	-0.1359	0.0503	-0.1138	0.0700	-0.0275	0.1141	0.2997	-0.0793	-0.0324	0.0353
2	0.1756	0.1157	0.3125	0.0847	0.1611	0.0259	-0.0612	0.0871	0.2765	0.0825
3	-0.1557	-0.0464	-0.1350	0.1231	-0.0527	-0.0127	0.1557	0.1358	0.0303	0.1133
4	-0.0273	0.0194	0.1085	0.1619	0.1849	-0.0114	0.1115	0.0230	-0.0105	-0.0782
5	-0.0034	0.0223	0.2533	0.0150	0.2596	-0.0271	0.0260	0.0926	0.2137	-0.1345
6	-0.0641	0.0158	0.0352	0.2146	-0.0052	0.0663	0.1630	0.0062	-0.0605	0.0189
7	-0.1738	0.0486	0.0666	0.1266	0.0470	-0.0055	0.2716	0.1089	0.0897	-0.1074
8	0.1934	0.3726	0.0217	-0.1154	0.0653	-0.0098	-0.0172	-0.0978	0.0186	0.0434
9	-0.1160	-0.0843	-0.0876	0.0893	0.0357	0.0736	0.1568	0.0724	0.0552	-0.0197
10	-0.0029	-0.0318	0.0129	0.0653	0.0615	-0.0874	0.0203	0.0981	-0.0318	0.1167
11	-0.0409	-0.1525	0.0674	-0.0818	0.0469	-0.0591	0.0024	0.0274	0.1294	-0.0482
12	-0.0037	0.0553	0.1060	0.1538	0.1018	-0.0135	0.0908	0.0962	0.0549	0.0180
13	-0.1896	-0.1241	-0.1038	-0.0960	-0.1301	-0.0674	-0.0047	-0.0598	0.0690	0.0975
14	-0.0365	-0.0460	0.1503	0.0966	0.0661	0.1251	0.0689	0.0024	0.0046	-0.1005
15	-0.2064	0.0477	0.0889	0.0945	-0.0212	0.0996	0.3155	0.0970	0.1093	0.1140
16	-0.0863	-0.0141	0.1858	0.0272	0.0224	-0.0463	0.0482	0.1552	0.0587	0.1060
17	-0.0711	0.0869	-0.0690	-0.0190	0.2375	0.0793	0.1474	0.0887	0.0837	-0.0403
18	-0.0259	-0.0671	-0.0636	-0.0113	0.0264	0.0605	0.1509	-0.0148	-0.0005	-0.1176
19	-0.0859	-0.0647	-0.0857	0.1073	0.0089	-0.0304	0.1202	0.0872	0.1749	-0.0205
20	-0.1083	-0.0480	0.1220	0.0058	0.0167	-0.0791	-0.0647	0.2101	0.0652	0.1599
21	-0.0294	0.0101	0.1121	0.0841	0.1601	0.2106	0.1117	-0.0421	-0.0429	-0.0620
22	-0.0434	0.1002	0.0628	0.0846	0.1192	0.0145	0.1579	0.0939	0.0425	0.1335
23	0.0847	0.0278	-0.0594	0.0420	0.0411	0.1137	0.2739	-0.0105	0.0820	0.0083
24	-0.0173	0.0399	0.0307	0.1363	-0.0476	0.1417	0.3255	-0.0445	0.0758	0.0680
25	-0.0826	-0.0349	0.0596	0.1204	-0.1003	0.0216	-0.0522	-0.0704	0.0070	-0.0383
26	-0.0593	0.0642	-0.1478	0.0225	-0.0087	-0.0846	0.1124	-0.0253	-0.0433	0.0789
27	-0.0586	-0.1186	-0.0606	-0.0119	-0.1227	-0.0064	-0.0160	-0.0475	0.0711	0.1320
28	0.0199	-0.0275	-0.0550	0.0364	-0.0095	0.0369	0.1514	0.0848	0.0690	0.1259
29	0.1020	0.0718	0.1675	0.0907	0.1777	0.1589	0.0488	0.0464	0.1078	0.0471
30	0.0151	0.0937	0.0575	0.1613	0.0557	0.0842	0.1550	-0.1114	0.0857	-0.0656
31	-0.0071	-0.0122	0.4591	0.0975	0.1981	0.0416	0.0797	0.0159	0.1293	-0.0313
32	0.0416	0.0584	0.2622	-0.0155	0.2413	-0.0768	-0.0281	0.0514	0.0547	0.0796
33	-0.0273	-0.0662	0.2058	0.1104	0.1414	0.0938	0.0669	0.1479	0.2220	-0.0133
34	-0.1654	-0.0481	-0.0382	0.0514	0.0462	0.1180	0.1110	-0.0102	0.0382	-0.0211

35	0.1114	0.0830	0.1342	0.1385	0.0213	-0.0784	0.0479	-0.0696	-0.1103	0.0103
36	0.0757	0.0229	0.0850	0.2175	0.0471	0.1378	0.0064	0.2444	0.0292	-0.0934
37	0.1902	0.1051	0.1134	0.0100	-0.0525	0.1524	0.0617	0.0224	-0.0787	-0.0434
38	-0.0989	0.0039	0.0936	0.0121	-0.1174	0.0854	0.0614	0.1691	-0.1080	-0.1367
39	-0.0623	-0.1242	-0.1286	-0.1298	-0.0624	-0.1555	-0.0442	-0.1485	-0.2048	-0.1846
40	-0.0337	0.0876	0.0141	0.1054	0.0957	-0.0832	0.0859	-0.0140	0.0246	-0.0037
41	0.0610	0.2154	-0.0571	0.0348	0.0432	-0.0536	0.0772	-0.0634	-0.0825	-0.1589
42	0.2056	0.0006	0.1198	-0.0769	0.0520	0.0057	0.1502	-0.0778	0.0094	-0.0737
43	-0.0493	0.0461	0.0114	0.1843	0.0152	0.1653	0.1322	0.1677	0.0346	0.0116
44	0.0762	0.1919	-0.0891	0.2169	0.1803	0.1360	0.0730	0.1893	-0.0416	-0.0926
45	0.0803	0.1684	-0.0289	0.1808	0.1854	0.0431	0.1323	0.0098	0.0795	0.0706
46	0.1258	0.1666	0.0708	0.1770	-0.0122	-0.0868	0.1050	-0.0756	0.0231	-0.0971
47	0.0499	0.1669	-0.0098	-0.0093	0.1221	0.1521	0.0769	0.2257	-0.0263	-0.1002
48	0.0562	-0.0305	0.0367	-0.0024	-0.1611	-0.0438	0.0322	-0.0795	0.1103	0.0194
49	0.0283	0.1596	0.0021	0.0762	-0.0396	0.1615	0.1107	0.2410	0.0386	-0.0511
50	0.0613	0.1282	0.1226	-0.0382	-0.1828	-0.1481	-0.0060	-0.0070	-0.0235	-0.0665
51	-0.0115	0.1856	0.1311	0.0690	-0.0955	0.0712	-0.0213	0.0398	-0.0817	0.0841
52	-0.0139	-0.1078	0.0512	0.2264	0.1452	0.0072	0.0533	0.0414	0.0895	-0.0068
53	0.0053	-0.0396	-0.0076	0.1780	0.1135	0.0555	-0.0921	0.0185	0.0445	-0.0785
54	-0.0051	0.0844	0.0637	-0.0085	-0.0210	0.2842	0.0542	0.1233	0.0998	0.0407
55	0.1249	0.0951	0.1145	0.2004	-0.0290	-0.0901	0.0916	0.0193	-0.0274	-0.0772
56	-0.0353	0.2342	0.1665	0.0436	0.0003	0.2853	0.1835	0.1850	-0.0057	-0.1406
57	-0.1164	0.0895	-0.0378	0.1858	0.1092	0.0339	0.1217	0.0804	-0.1293	-0.1183
58	-0.0444	0.0391	0.0053	-0.0013	0.0766	0.0683	-0.0482	0.1050	0.0221	-0.0109
59	0.0602	-0.0240	0.1310	0.0798	-0.0357	-0.0698	0.1338	-0.0074	-0.0625	-0.0281
60	-0.1147	0.0423	-0.0222	-0.0371	-0.0329	0.1684	-0.0747	0.0996	0.4176	0.2970
61	-0.1727	0.0254	0.0330	-0.0691	-0.0688	0.1301	-0.0442	-0.0465	0.2332	1.0000

Table 4-4
Correlation Coefficients for Securities with Minimally Correlated Residuals

Number	Min. R	Security Code		Security Code		Industry Codes	
1	-0.3935	380	CONSOLIDATED EDISON CO NY	195	BETHLEHEM STEEL CORP	492	331
2	-0.3009	1361	STANDARD OIL OF NEW JERSEY	11	ADMIRAL CORPORATION	291	365
3	-0.2944	1361	STANDARD OIL OF NEW JERSEY	1179	PHILIP MORRIS INC	291	211
4	-0.2611	1181	PHILLIPS PETROLEUM	629	GENERAL MOTORS	291	371
5	-0.2599	1239	REYNOLDS METALS	253	CIT FINANCIAL	333	614
6	-0.2578	1358	STANDARD OIL OF CALIF	831	JONES & LAUGHLIN STEEL CORP	291	331
7	-0.2480	1540	US STEEL	1358	STANDARD OIL OF CALIF	331	291
8	-0.2451	1352	SPERRY RAND CORP	848	KENNECOTT COPPER	366	333
9	-0.2281	1361	STANDARD OIL OF NEW JERSEY	508	EASTMAN KODAK	291	383
10	-0.2245	1322	SKELLY OIL	629	GENERAL MOTORS	291	371
11	-0.2240	629	GENERAL MOTORS	508	EASTMAN KODAK	371	383
12	-0.2226	1361	STANDARD OIL OF NEW JERSEY	1200	PROCTOR & GAMBLE CO	291	284
13	-0.2223	1432	TEXACO	1234	REPUBLIC STEEL CORP	291	331
14	-0.2201	629	GENERAL MOTORS	487	DOW CHEMICAL CO	371	281
15	-0.2195	1358	STANDARD OIL OF CALIF	1234	REPUBLIC STEEL CORP	291	331
16	-0.2181	997	CONTINENTAL OIL	629	GENERAL MOTORS	291	371
17	-0.2179	1432	TEXACO	11	ADMIRAL CORPORATION	291	365
18	-0.2148	1335	SOUTHERN CO	793	INTERNATIONAL PAPER	491	262
19	-0.2100	1361	STANDARD OIL OF NEW JERSEY	623	GENERAL ELECTRIC	291	361
20	-0.2080	997	CONTINENTAL OIL	11	ADMIRAL CORPORATION	291	365
21	-0.2064	998	GULF OIL CORP	122	ARMOUR & CO	291	201
22	-0.2059	1359	STANDARD OIL OF INDIANA	623	GENERAL ELECTRIC	291	361
23	-0.2058	1432	TEXACO	863	KRESGE SS	291	533
24	-0.2057	629	GENERAL MOTORS	629	GENERAL MOTORS	333	371
25	-0.2049	806	INTERNATIONAL NICKEL	629	GENERAL MOTORS	366	371
26	-0.2048	1008	MISSION CORP	629	GENERAL MOTORS	671	371
27	-0.2046	1361	STANDARD OIL OF NEW JERSEY	1242	REYNOLDS TOBACCO	291	211
28	-0.2044	1358	STANDARD OIL OF CALIF	1305	SHARON STEEL CORP	291	331
29	-0.2038	1432	TEXACO	1099	NORTHWEST AIRLINES	291	451
30	-0.2028	724	HERCULES POWDER CO	629	GENERAL MOTORS	289	371

31	-0.2018	1359	STANDARD OIL OF INDIANA	253	CIT FINANCIAL	291	614
32	-0.1980	333	CHRYSLER CORP	70	AMERICAN HOME PRODUCTS	371	283
33	-0.1963	1308	SHELL OIL CO	508	EASTMAN KODAK	291	383
34	-0.1955	1361	STANDARD OIL OF NEW JERSEY	119	ARMCO STEEL CORP	291	331
35	-0.1946	1540	US STEEL	1008	MISSION CORP	331	671
36	-0.1944	1361	STANDARD OIL OF NEW JERSEY	1298	SEARS ROEBUCK	291	532
37	-0.1941	1540	US STEEL	1432	TEXACO	331	291
38	-0.1941	1452	TIMKEN ROLLER BEARING	1157	PENNSYLVANIA POWER & LIGHT	356	491
39	-0.1938	510	EATON MANUFACTURING CO	380	CONSOLIDATED EDISON CO NY	371	492
40	-0.1929	683	GREYHOUND CORP	629	GENERAL MOTORS	413	371
41	-0.1924	1358	STANDARD OIL OF CALIF	195	BETHLEHEM STEEL CORP	291	331
42	-0.1911	1361	STANDARD OIL OF NEW JERSEY	1115	OTIS ELEVATOR	291	352
43	-0.1897	1358	STANDARD OIL OF CALIF	87	AMERICAN RADIATOR CO	291	343
44	-0.1896	998	GULF OIL CORP	98	AT&T CO	291	481
45	-0.1893	1322	SKELLY OIL	1298	SEARS ROEBUCK	291	532
46	-0.1888	1531	US LINES CO NJ	497	DUPONT	441	281
47	-0.1878	1358	STANDARD OIL OF CALIF	119	ARMCO STEEL CORP	291	331
48	-0.1860	303	CERRO CORP	253	CIT FINANCIAL	333	614
49	-0.1860	1361	STANDARD OIL OF NEW JERSEY	1335	SOUTHERN CO	291	491
50	-0.1852	782	IBM CORP	629	GENERAL MOTORS	357	371

Table 4-5
Correlation Coefficients for Securities with Highly Correlated Residuals

Number	Max. R	Security Code		Security Code		Industry Codes	
1	0.7382	1322	SKELLY OIL	1008	MISSION CORP	291	671
2	0.6647	1234	REPUBLIC STEEL CORP	831	JONES & LAUGHLIN STEEL CORP	331	331
3	0.5983	1540	US STEEL	831	JONES & LAUGHLIN STEEL CORP	331	331
4	0.5974	1540	US STEEL	1234	REPUBLIC STEEL CORP	331	331
5	0.5858	1540	US STEEL	195	BETHLEHEM STEEL CORP	331	331
6	0.5701	831	JONES & LAUGHLIN STEEL CORP	195	BETHLEHEM STEEL CORP	331	331
7	0.5456	1540	US STEEL	119	ARMCO STEEL CORP	331	331
8	0.5360	1234	REPUBLIC STEEL CORP	119	ARMCO STEEL CORP	331	331
9	0.5343	661	GOODYEAR TIRE AND RUBBER	572	FIRESTONE TIRE & RUBBER CO	301	301
10	0.5259	1305	SHARON STEEL CORP	831	JONES & LAUGHLIN STEEL CORP	331	331
11	0.5197	1432	TEXACO	1358	STANDARD OIL OF CALIF	291	291
12	0.5124	831	JONES & LAUGHLIN STEEL CORP	119	ARMCO STEEL CORP	331	331
13	0.5087	1234	REPUBLIC STEEL CORP	195	BETHLEHEM STEEL CORP	331	331
14	0.4805	1322	SKELLY OIL	997	CONTINENTAL OIL	291	291
15	0.4646	1432	TEXACO	1361	STANDARD OIL OF NEW JERSEY	291	291
16	0.4632	793	INTERNATIONAL PAPER	426	CROWN ZELLERBACH CORP	262	262
17	0.4591	1020	MONSANTO CO	487	DOW CHEMICAL CO	281	281
18	0.4553	1305	SHARON STEEL CORP	1234	REPUBLIC STEEL CORP	331	331
19	0.4549	1242	REYNOLDS TOBACCO	1179	PHILIP MORRIS INC	211	211
20	0.4528	1359	STANDARD OIL OF INDIANA	997	CONTINENTAL OIL	291	291
21	0.4439	661	GOODYEAR TIRE AND RUBBER	659	GOODRICH BF	301	301
22	0.4399	1359	STANDARD OIL OF INDIANA	1322	SKELLY OIL	291	291
23	0.4384	1359	STANDARD OIL OF INDIANA	40	AMERADA PETROLEUM CORP	291	131
24	0.4377	1358	STANDARD OIL OF CALIF	998	GULF OIL CORP	291	291
25	0.4356	1308	SHELL OIL CO	997	CONTINENTAL OIL	291	291
26	0.4284	1322	SKELLY OIL	1308	SHELL OIL CO	291	291
27	0.4245	1361	STANDARD OIL OF NEW JERSEY	1358	STANDARD OIL OF CALIF	291	291
28	0.4230	831	JONES & LAUGHLIN STEEL CORP	21	ALLEGHENY LUDLUM STEEL	331	331
29	0.4216	1234	REPUBLIC STEEL CORP	21	ALLEGHENY LUDLUM STEEL	331	331
30	0.4207	1305	SHARON STEEL CORP	195	BETHLEHEM STEEL CORP	331	331

31	0.4176	1008	MISSION CORP	997	CONTINENTAL OIL	671	291
32	0.4169	1322	SKELLY OIL	40	AMERADA PETROLEUM CORP	291	131
33	0.4119	1361	STANDARD OIL OF NEW JERSEY	998	GULF OIL CORP	291	291
34	0.4096	1359	STANDARD OIL OF INDIANA	1358	STANDARD OIL OF CALIF	291	131
35	0.4082	997	CONTINENTAL OIL	40	AMERADA PETROLEUM CORP	291	131
36	0.4081	195	BETHLEHEM STEEL CORP	119	ARMCO STEEL CORP	331	331
37	0.4043	1322	SKELLY OIL	1181	PHILLIPS PETROLEUM	291	291
38	0.4032	1308	SHELL OIL CO	1181	PHILLIPS PETROLEUM	291	291
39	0.4027	1482	UNION CARBIDE CORP	487	DOW CHEMICAL CO	287	281
40	0.4027	1358	STANDARD OIL OF CALIF	1008	MISSION CORP	291	671
41	0.3962	1181	PHILLIPS PETROLEUM	997	CONTINENTAL OIL	291	291
42	0.3945	1540	US STEEL	1305	SHARON STEEL CORP	331	331
43	0.3940	1432	TEXACO	1008	MISSION CORP	291	671
44	0.3914	1432	TEXACO	998	GULF OIL CORP	291	291
45	0.3892	119	ARMCO STEEL CORP	21	ALLEGHENY LUDLUM STEEL	331	331
46	0.3881	1181	PHILLIPS PETROLEUM	1008	MISSION CORP	291	671
47	0.3850	1359	STANDARD OIL OF INDIANA	1181	PHILLIPS PETROLEUM	291	291
48	0.3833	1536	US RUBBER	661	GOODYEAR TIRE AND RUBBER	301	301
49	0.3798	1358	STANDARD OIL OF CALIF	997	CONTINENTAL OIL	291	291
50	0.3775	629	GENERAL MOTORS	333	CHRYSLER CORP	371	371

Table 4-6
Securities with Nonmatching Industry Codes (from among the 100 highest residual correlations)

No.	Correlation of Residuals	Name		Industry Codes	Name		Industry Codes
1	0.3306	Jones & Laughlin Steel	331		Chicago Milwaukee R.R.	401	
2	0.3255	Northwest Air Lines	451		Chicago Milwaukee R.R.	401	
3	0.3199	Simmons Company	251		S.S. Kresge	533	
4	0.3155	Northwest Airlines	451		Armour & Company	201	
5	0.3061	Jones & Laughlin Steel	331		General Refractories	325	
6	0.3016	U.S. Steel	331		General Refractories	325	
7	0.2997	Northwest Airlines	451		ACF Industries Inc.	374	
8	0.2948	Sharon Steel Corp.	331		General Refractories	325	
9	0.2944	International Paper	262		Dupont	281	
10	0.2904	Cerro Corp.	333		Allis Chalmers Mfg.	352	
11	0.2897	Timken Roller Bearing	356		Rockwell Standard Corp.	371	

Morris; General Motors with Chrysler Corporation; Phelps Dodge with Kennecott Copper; International Harvester with Deere & Co.; S.S. Kresge with Allied Stores; and United States Gypsum with Johns-Manville. Even among the eleven pairs of securities noted in Table 4-6 as exceptions to the observation that the most highly correlated residuals occur among companies within the same industry, there are strong industry overtones. Witness the pairing effected by highly correlated residuals of General Refractories with the steel companies or of Timken Roller Bearing with Rockwell Standard. It is clear that of the 4950 correlations among market model residuals for this sample of 100 securities, there is no discernable industry influence at low levels of residual correlation. It is equally clear that the industry factor plays a significant role among those securities with highly correlated market-model residuals.

The selection of 100 as the number of both high and low correlations to be closely examined was rather arbitrary, since these represent only a small fraction of the 4950 correlation coefficients generated among the market-model residuals. It is also limiting to the extent that a significant number of the 100 sample securities do not happen to be represented among these two hundred high and low values and therefore do not appear on these lists. Steels, oils, and chemicals appear to comprise a substantial portion of the list; and most companies in these industries, because of the very nature of the list, appear many times.[5] Thus, it may be that while the residuals of companies within these few industries are highly correlated, it may not be true that this conditional dependence exists across the full sample of 100 securities.

In order to test this possibility, each security in the sample was paired with the one security that its residuals were most highly correlated with and with the one security that its residuals were least correlated with. The results can be portrayed graphically if we arrange the securities in the correlation matrix by industry. This has been done and the location of each security's most highly correlated partner in the correlation matrix has been plotted. These are shown in Figure 4-1. This figure is simply a picture of the 100 X 100 correlation matrix for the residuals of the sample securities, with an indication of the location of the other *one* security in the sample that each security's residuals are most highly correlated with. Plotted points are shown only for securities whose two-digit industry code appeared in the sample of 100 at least twice. For example, Endicott Johnson Corp., Industry Code 314 is not shown, since there is no other company in the sample in the 31 class. In line with the previous discussion, both Mission Corp. and Amerada are ordered in the matrix among the petroleum refining companies. Figure 4-2 shows the same information for the minimum residual correlations of each security.

If there is no systematic influence affecting the residuals, if they are truly

---

[5] If U.S. Steel is highly correlated with Republic Steel and with Armco Steel, Republic and Armco will also appear again in the list as highly correlated themselves.

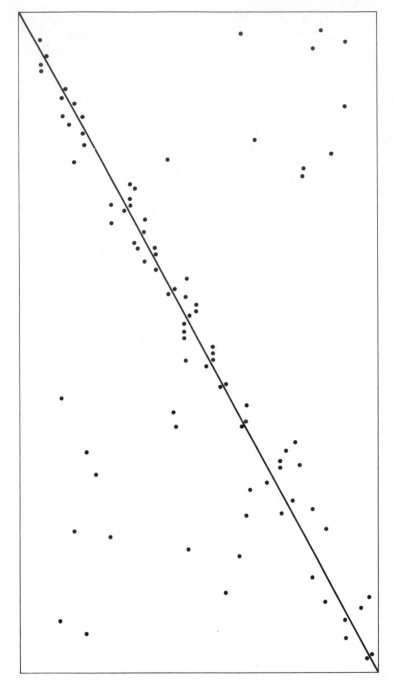

Figure 4–1. Correlation Matrix: Locus of Maximum Correlations.

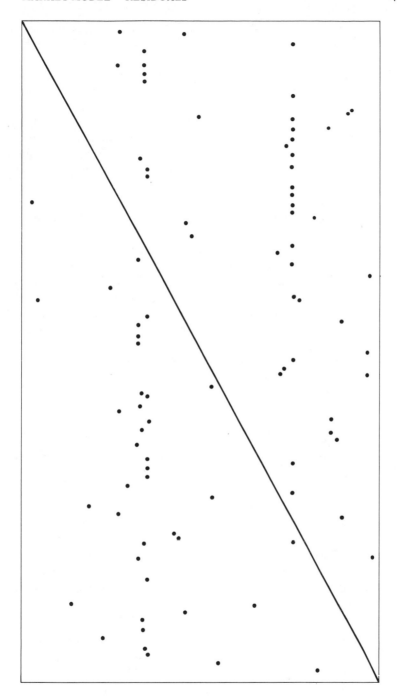

Figure 4–2. Correlation Matrix: Locus of Minimum Correlations.

independent, the plotted points should appear randomly scattered regardless of the ordering of the securities in the matrix. And there should be no noticeable difference between the figure depicting the plotted maximums and the figure showing the plotted minimums. If, however, there is an underlying systematic element and if it is related to industry structure, the ordering of securities by industry in the matrix would cause the plotted maximums to cluster around the diagonal and the plotted minimums to shun the diagonal. (Actually if the sample includes six companies in one industry it would be possible to have a plotted maximum five units away from the diagonal. The diagonal referred to is really a range, the width of the number of companies in a particular industry. However, it is felt that since these ranges in most cases are rather small, this imperfection does not detract significantly from the presentation. To draw the limits of this range for each industry on the matrix unnecessarily complicates the portrayal.)

Figure 4-1, which shows the location of those securities whose residuals are most highly correlated with each of the sample securities in turn, has a very discernible clustering about the diagonal. In fact, a band twelve units[6] wide drawn around the diagonal includes all but twenty-three companies. The points also tend to run the full length of the diagonal, indicating that the correlation of yield residuals is not just peculiar to a few key industries but, in fact, occurs over the full range of industry codes included in the sample. Other notable pairs of securities that occur in this particular analysis include American Can Co. most highly correlated with Continental Can Co.; AT&T with General Telephone & Electronics; Burroughs Corporation with Sperry Rand: CIT Financial with Household Finance and Parke Davis with Abbot Laboratories. The complete listing including the correlation coefficient for each pair of securities is included in the Appendix.

Figure 4-2 shows similar data plotted for paired securities with minimum correlations. Its most striking feature is the complete lack of points plotted near the diagonal. A twelve-unit band around the diagonal includes only nine plotted points.

The results portrayed in Figures 4-1 and 4-2 for this sample do strongly suggest an underlying systematic factor positively related to industry groupings.

In summary, it appears that there is dependence among security returns that is not fully accounted for by a single market factor and that this dependence occurs at least to some degree along industry lines. In an attempt to account for this observed dependence, Chapter 5 discusses the use of three naive multi-index models which include industry factors as well as the market factor.

------

[6] The maximum number of companies with the same two-digit industry code within the sample.

5 Tests of a Multi-Index Model

We have discussed the point that on both theoretical and practical grounds there is reason to question the validity of the one-factor market model. Theoretically the assumption that security returns are related only through a common market factor and the companion assumption concerning the nature of the covariance structure are questionable. On more practical grounds, portfolio managers contend that the single-factor market model is oversimplified; investors recognize security subgroups and make decisions on the basis of industry groupings as well as on the basis of less formal "blue chip," "defensive," "growth," and "cyclical" categories.

For these reasons and because of the strong evidence relating to industry groupings (presented in the previous chapter), it appears worthwhile to examine at least one simple multifactor model before moving on to the final phase of the research, dealing with the use of a particular model to assess the risk exposure of actual mutual-fund portfolios.

In the context of our previous discussion about systematic risk a multi-index model does not introduce any new conceptual difficulties. Recalling that systematic risk is simply that portion of the uncertainty about a security's expected return that is not unique to the particular security, in the use of a multi-index model, vis-a-vis the single index market model, we have simply expanded the breadth of the systematic element so that it also includes elements common to industry groupings. Stated in another manner, elements of uncertainty that are unique to securities given the market, but that are not unique to individual securities when collected in industry groups, are summarized and also made part of the systematic risk factor.

The Proposed Model

The model proposed is basically just an expansion of the single-index market model so that it also includes industry indexes. It proposes that the returns of the ith security are related not only to the market index but also to a number of industry indexes, i.e.,

$$\widetilde{R}_{it} = a_i + b_i \widetilde{R}_{mt} + {}_1 b_{i\,1} \widetilde{I}_t + {}_2 b_{i\,2} \widetilde{I}_t + \ldots + {}_n b_{i\,n} \widetilde{I}_t + \widetilde{e}_{it}$$

47

where

$\widetilde{R}_{it}$ = $\log(\widetilde{P}_{i(t+n)}/P_{it})$ and $\widetilde{P}_{i(t+\tau)}$ is the price of security i at time $(t + \tau)$ adjusted for dividends and other distributions; while P_{it} is the price for security i at time t

τ = a time interval of one month

$\widetilde{R}_{mt}$ = $\log(\widetilde{M}_{(t+\tau)}/M_t)$ and $\widetilde{M}_{(t+\tau)}$ is the level of the Standard & Poor's Composite 500 Stock Index adjusted for distributions, at time $(t + \tau)$ while M_t is the level of the Standard & Poor's Composite 500 Stock Index at time t

$\widetilde{e}_{it}$ = a residual; normally distributed with expectation of 0; $\mathrm{cov}(\widetilde{e}_i, \widetilde{R}_{mt})$ = 0; $\mathrm{cov}(\widetilde{e}_i, {}_n\widetilde{I}_t) = 0$ for $n = 1,n$; and $\mathrm{cov}(\widetilde{e}_i, \widetilde{e}_j) = 0$ for $i \neq j$

$${}_n\widetilde{I}_t = \log\left\{\left[\sum_{k=1}^{m} \frac{{}_n\widetilde{P}_{k(t+\tau)}}{{}_nP_{kt}}\right]/(m-1)\right\} \text{ for } k \neq i$$

i.e., the log of the mean price relative computed using the m securities in the nth industry. To avoid the overspecification possible in industries with few securities, the ith security was eliminated from its respective index when this model was used to determine the parameters of the ith security. The mean price relative for this index was then based on $(m - 1)$ securities.

Each of the indexes constructed included *all* of the securities on the CRSP tape in that industry class.[1] If the industry code of a security changed during the 246 month interval over which the indexes were constructed, the appropriate indexes were adjusted to reflect this change. And as already noted, the indexes were constructed to allow for the elimination of any given security, included in the index, when the index was used as an independent variable in a model where the given security was the dependent variable.

The intent of any index is to provide a summary measure that fairly represents the activity of its components. However, indexes can be constructed in a wide variety of ways. Consider the differences among five indexes that were designed to portray daily stock market activity:

The Dow Jones Industrial Average is an unweighted average of the prices of

---

[1] The CRSP tape includes 1640 securities in the December 1945–June 1966 interval. Each of these was used as part of an index for the length of time it appeared on the tape and for the length of time it was identified as being part of a particular industry.

a sample of thirty New York Stock Exchange common stocks. Stock dividends and splits are accounted for by adjusting a divisor.

The Standard & Poor's Composite 500 Stock Index is a weighted average of the prices of a sample of 500 New York Stock Exchange common stocks. The weights are the number of shares outstanding of each stock in the sample. The index is determined relative to a base of 10 computed for the years 1941-1943.

The New York Stock Exchange Composite Index is similar to the Standard & Poor's 500 in that it too is a weighted average of stock prices. However, it includes all of the common stock listed on the New York Stock Exchange. It is computed relative to a base of 50 for December 31, 1965.

The American Stock Exchange Index is the sum of the previous day's index and an unweighted arithmetic average of the price changes of securities traded on a given day. The initial price was established at 16.88 on April 29, 1966.

The Over-the-Counter Index is a simple arithmetic average of the prices of thirty-five over-the-counter securities.

Each of these involves compromises made originally because of ease of computation, the nature of the universe to be summarized, or the availability of data—as do the industry indexes described above. Because of time and cost constraints, it was essential that indexes be constructed with data already available. It was also essential that each security be capable of being assigned to its respective industry with a minimum of effort. And, although the indexes might have been more representative had they been weighted by the outstanding shares of each component security, it was not considered feasible to do so—again because of data availability considerations.

These shortcomings cause the industry indexes employed not to be representative of the component securities, and to that extent the model will fail to account for portions of the systematic elements we hope to isolate. Unfortunately, it is not possible to measure this factor or to make adjustments for it.

Three naive versions of the multi-index model specified were tested. Each employed the market index and seven industry indexes. The first used industry indexes based on the seven one-digit industrial classifications (industry codes 100 to 700). The second version included seven industry indexes selected from among all the possible *two-digit* industry class indexes that could be constructed given the securities listed on the CRSP tape. Similarly, the third version was based on seven industry indexes selected from among all the possible *three-digit* industry class indexes that could be constructed from the CRSP data.

Although this approach appears justified based on the results presented in the previous chapter, its naivete presents some very real complications. For while these formulations of the model are expected to capture more of the underlying systematic factors influencing $\widetilde{R}_i$, there can still be no assurance that all nonunique elements will have been isolated. Also, it is very difficult, if not impossible, to construct industry indexes that are themselves jointly independent. For example, the mean correlation among pairs of indexes constructed on the basis of ninety-nine separate three-digit industry classes, was 0.5694, while the range extended from a minimum of 0.2138 to a maximum of 0.9222. Thus, in using three-digit indexes, the smallest correlation that could occur among the industry indexes is 0.2138. But note also, these two particular indexes themselves are correlated with the market index, with correlation coefficients of 0.4459 and 0.4753. In fact, of the ninety-nine indexes, the one index least correlated with the market had a correlation of 0.45 with the market index. Although factor analysis could, of course, be used to construct jointly independent indexes, the problem then arises of relating these indexes to familiar real-world phenomena, which is of course essential if we are to forecast their future values.

Finally, since one of our basic concerns is the applicability of these research results, we must note that a multi-index model greatly increases the number of assessments required by the portfolio manager.

The ultimate model would consist of perhaps three or four independent indexes that could explain all or most all of the systematic portion of the variance of individual security returns, and require a relatively small number of assessments by the portfolio manager. No effort will be made to identify such a model in this research. The purpose of this chapter is primarily to examine the correlation among residuals after applying the three versions of the specified multi-index model.

Testing the Model

The procedures used for testing each version of the model will be described and the comparative results, together with similar findings obtained for the single-index market model, will be presented. The first formulation, that based on one-digit industry codes was the simplest. Each of the seven indexes was computed and each security in the sample of one hundred was run through the model. The residuals were saved and the 100 × 100 correlation matrix of residuals was computed.

The tests of the model based on two-digit and three-digit industry indexes were more complex. Seven indexes had to be selected from among forty-six possible two-digit industry classes for trial two, and from ninety-nine potential three-digit industry classes for trial three.[2]

A description of the procedure used to select the seven two-digit indexes

---

[2] This includes all two-digit and three-digit classes for which at least two observations (securities) were available in each of the 246 months over which the indexes were computed.

for trial two follows. Briefly the correlation matrix was searched for two or three indexes that were highly correlated with as many of the remainder as possible. Two such indexes were found: industry code 35, *Machinery*; and industry code 20, *Food and kindred products*. All but thirteen of the forty-six original indexes had correlations in excess of 0.70 with one of these two. So that if these two were included in the model, it was not unreasonable to eliminate the others. The five remaining indexes were selected from the remaining thirteen using the following criteria:

1. That the index have sufficient observations (at least five) so that its movement could not be attributed to the peculiarities of one security.
2. That some breadth be achieved over the range of the seven industrial classes.
3. That some consideration be given to obtaining a variety of indexes in terms of the other groupings previously discussed: defensive, cyclical, etc.
4. That the indexes selected be relatively uncorrelated themselves.

The seven final indexes and their correlation matrix along with the correlation of each with the Standard & Poor's 500 are shown in Table 5-1.

Although a similar procedure might have been used to select seven three-digit industry indexes from among the ninety-nine possible, it was decided to select those indexes that had the greatest likelihood of reducing the correlation among the residuals for the sample of one hundred securities. Consequently, the seven indexes chosen were those that carried the same industrial code as the greatest number of securities within the sample of one hundred. These are shown in Table 5-2.

Admittedly this version of the model is unrealistic and artificial. Followed to its logical conclusion it would suggest a model which includes a three-digit industry index for each security under consideration. The prospect of working with a model with up to ninety-nine separate industry indexes is certainly less than appealing and hardly practical. In this instance, however, the employment of the model with indexes selected in this manner can provide an indication of the maximum amount of success we may achieve in isolating systematic industry elements using this approach.

Findings

If the multi-index models postulated are of any value in accounting for the systematic elements observed in the residuals generated by the market model, we would expect the following: (1) The distribution of the correlation coefficients should be less skewed toward the positive side and approach a symmetric distribution. (2) The mean correlation of residuals should be progressively reduced and approach 0; although this may not be apparent since after applying just the

Table 5–1
Correlation Among Selected Two-Digit Industry Indexes

Industry	Number		00 1	10 2	20 3	31 4	35 5	45 6	58 7	61 8
Standard & Poor's 500	00	1	1.0	0.6161	0.8064	0.5994	0.8762	0.5881	0.5794	0.6410
Metal mining	10	2		1.0	0.6862	0.5021	0.6670	0.5184	0.4885	0.4294
Food and kindred products	20	3			1.0	0.6679	0.8653	0.6212	0.6423	0.6632
Leather and leather products	31	4				1.0	0.6096	0.4234	0.5017	0.4339
Machinery	35	5					1.0	0.6917	0.6362	0.6207
Air transportation	45	6						1.0	0.4153	0.3577
Eating and drinking places	58	7							1.0	0.5174
Credit agencies	61	8								1.0

Table 5-2
Three-Digit Industry Indexes

Industry Code	Industry	Number of Sample Securities in Industry
281	Industrial chemicals	5
291	Petroleum refining	9
301	Tires and inner tubes	4
331	Steel works, and rolling and finishing mills	7
333	Smelting and refining of nonferrous metals	5
352	Farm machinery and equipment	5
371	Motor vehicles and motor vehicle equipment	4
	Total	39

single-index model, the mean correlation is already near 0. (3) More of the variance of security prices should be explained by the model thereby increasing values of the coefficient of determination, R^2, and reducing the amount of variance unique to each security.

If industry factors are important at all, trial three should result in the most significant change in the structure of the correlation matrix. Given a seven industry model and the particular sample of one hundred securities, using a criterion for index selection based on sample composition *ensures* a dramatic change in the structure of the correlation matrix, *if* industry indexes, as computed herein, are representative of the systematic industry factors discovered in the previous chapter.

We shall also report on a χ^2 test conducted to test for independence among the residuals $\tilde{e}_i$. This was done for the single-index model as well as for the three versions of the multi-index model. Morrison describes a χ^2 statistic for accepting or rejecting a hypothesis of independence at a specified significance level.[3] The test statistic is

$$\chi^2 = (N - 1 - \frac{2p + 5}{6}) \left(\sum_{i<j} \sum r_{ij}^2 \right)$$

where the summation of the squared correlation coefficients extends over the $\frac{1}{2}[p(p-1)]$ correlations in the upper portion of the correlation matrix. And where the term $N-1$ is attributable to the N independent observation vectors in the sample. For a test level we should accept the hypothesis of independence if

$$\chi^2 < \chi^2_\alpha; \frac{1}{2}p(p-1)$$

Summary statistics are presented in Table 5-3.

---

[3] Donald F. Morrison, *Multi-Variate Statistical Methods* (New York: McGraw Hill, 1967).

Table 5-3
Tests of a Multi-Index Model: — Comparative Results

| Model | Mean Correlation | Range of Correlation Coefficient | | Sum ρ² | χ² | Mean Coefficients of Determination for Industry Class | | | | | | |
		Low	High			IC^b 100	IC 200	IC 300	IC 400	IC 500	IC 600	IC 700
Single index	0.0325	-0.3935	0.7382	60.5618	12,767.85	0.1398	0.3472	0.3805	0.2413	0.2458	0.2127	0.2147
Multi-index I	0.0090	-0.3747	0.6973	42.0994	8,875.94	0.2438a	0.4173a	0.4512a	0.3523a	0.3547a	0.2905a	0.4047a
Multi-index II	0.0126	-0.4023	0.7344	46.9874	9,906.90	0.2490a	0.4002a	0.4446a	0.3648a	0.3109a	0.3109a	0.3147
Multi-index III	0.0081	-0.4300	0.5163	31.5505	6,651.69	0.2478	0.4455a	0.4849a	0.3180	0.2900	0.3663	0.2875
Number of sample securities in this industry						2	33	46	9	6	3	1

a At least one index with this one-digit code was included in the model.
b IC = Industry Class.

Generally the mean correlation among residuals declines and there is some indication that the range of the correlation coefficient shifts toward the negative direction. Summed squared correlation coefficients and corresponding values of χ^2 decreased dramatically and are nearly halved in going from the single-index market model to the third version of the multi-index model. However χ^2 is not reduced to the point that would allow acceptance of the hypothesis of complete independence among residuals at the 0.05 level of significance. This is shown in another fashion if we look again at the pairs of securities whose residuals are highly correlated. While the correlation of residuals is generally lower, securities remain paired along industry lines. Sample data demonstrating this for the multi-index models are presented in the Appendix. This occurs because the industry indexes employed captured only a portion of the comovement of security prices within industries. There are further common factors influencing the price movements of securities within the same industry which were not accounted for by the particular industry proxies we employed.

The most surprising result is the outcome of the first and allegedly most naive version of the multi-index model, which is based on the one-digit industry indexes. This model performs better than the single-index market model in every respect and overall at least as well as the latter two versions of the multi-index model which utilize hand-picked industry indexes. Multi-index model III does increase the value of R^2 in the 200 and 300 industrial classes by 10 percentage points over the values noted for the single-index market model. But this should be expected given the contrived method used to select the industry indexes and given the fact that all seven industry indexes are included within these two classes. The slight difference between these 10 percentage points and the 7 percentage point increase for these two classes, achieved by multi-index model I, suggests that future effort might well be spent refining the naive model before attempting to define and work with more complex groupings of securities. For example, industry class 100 includes Agriculture, Forestry, and Fisheries; Mining; Contract Construction; and Manufacturing of Ordnance and Accessories. The quality of this index could be improved by assigning some of these industries to a different class. It might also be possible to combine some of these indexes in order to reduce the number of assessments required by the model and to achieve more independence among the resultant industry factors.

Summary

In summary, we noted that there is not complete conditional independence of security returns when just the single-index market model is used, and the task of identifying factors that explain residual comovement among these returns is not a simple one. Multi-index models can reduce the commonality shared within market subgroups, but at the cost of increased numbers of assessments and significantly more complex models.

6

The Measurement of Portfolio Risk-Exposure

The purpose of this chapter is to present the model that will be employed to measure portfolio risk levels; to discuss its advantages and limitations, and to relate it to models currently in use. The chapter also describes the nature of the research undertaken in the effort to apply this model, including a description of the sample portfolios employed and the limits that must be ascribed to the results. Chapter 7 presents and analyzes the results of applying the model to a number of mutual-fund portfolios during the 1960 decade.

Although we have tested simple versions of a multi-index model with some limited success, the complexities (noted in Chapter 5) involved in the use of such a model, together with the added inputs required from the portfolio manager, preclude its use at this time. In any event, there does appear to be some logic in pursuing this problem in somewhat smaller steps, for until this point in time researchers using the "market model" have assumed that both security systematic risk and portfolio systematic risk have not changed over time. This is the first attempt to work at the portfolio level with risk factors that are allowed to change. The joint efforts of introducing a multi-index model and nonstationary systematic risk elements on a multi-index basis, while of considerable interest, are beyond the scope of this research.

The Proposed Model

At the end of Chapter 2 we proposed a model for measuring portfolio systematic risk that had its basis in the single-index market model. The model states simply that at any given time the systematic risk of a portfolio is the weighted sum of the systematic risk elements of its component securities. Thus,

$$B_t = \sum_{j=1}^{n} X_{jt} b_j$$

where:

B_t = the portfolio systematic risk at time t

n = the number of securities in the portfolio

X_{jt} = the fraction of the portfolio invested in the jth security at time t

b_j = the systematic risk (volatility) of the jth security

We propose to employ this model in the following manner: (1) identify the securities within a portfolio; (2) compute the systematic risk, b_j, for each security using the market model; (3) weight the risk factor for each security by the proportion of the portfolio it represents; and (4) sum the weighted risk factors to arrive at the measure of portfolio systematic risk. Such a procedure permits the computation of the systematic risk of any portfolio at any appointed time. It allows the risk factor to change as portfolio composition changes. Using this model, the portfolio manager can simulate the risk effect of alternative investment decisions by introducing to his current portfolio the b_j coefficient and the proposed weighting of any security or combination of securities being considered for addition to or deletion from the portfolio. Pragmatically this measure has the advantage of sharing some of the principles involved in the concepts of relative strength and volatility already familiar to portfolio managers.

We can examine the behavior of portfolio risk levels over time in order to gain an insight into one aspect of a manager's performance, viz., his ability to predict market turns. If a portfolio manager is able to call major swings in the market successfully, we would expect that he would adjust the portfolio's risk level downward prior to market downturns and, conversely, increase it in anticipation of market upswings. By using the model to measure the volatility of a series of portfolios over time and relating the results to observed market action, we can comment on the portfolio manager's ability in this area.

We can also observe the manager's particular strategy for adjusting the portfolio's risk exposure. It is possible to compute a B_t net of cash and other liquid assets held in the portfolio and from these data make inferences about specific strategies employed to alter risk exposure. For example: In reducing risk reducing risk levels, to what extent does the portfolio manager rely on adjusting his cash position as opposed to shifting to less volatile securities? Is there a relationship between the particular strategy employed and the portfolio's size and/or level of systematic risk?

It is also possible now to determine if a portfolio manager is earning a rate of return consistent with the portfolio's level of systematic risk for short intervals of time, i.e., monthly, quarterly, or annually, in place of the ten-year periods used to date. And we can examine the continuing relationship between a portfolio's stated objective and its level of risk.

The research reported in Chapter 7 deals with the model's use and effectiveness in providing information in some of these areas.

Limitations

There are problems associated with the model, however; and these will be treated in the development of this chapter. Not the least of these is the matter of the stationarity of an individual security's systematic risk factor. In our tests of the stationarity of portfolio systematic risk we have made the implicit assumption that the systematic risk elements of individual securities, as measured within the single-index market model, are stationary. The results (noted in Chapter 3) together with Blume's findings suggest that this is not an unrealistic assumption in a portfolio context.[1]

Since our values of b_j, at this stage of the development of the theory, are based solely on historical data, one possible correction or refinement that might be employed, given an apparent lack of complete stationarity, would be to update the values of b_j. Updating in essence means computing a new value for b_j for example, each year, based on the most recent ten years of data.[2] If b_j is substantially stationary the factors would not change. If, however, they change gradually over time, although the computed value of b_j would always lag its true value, this estimate would be superior to the estimate made under the assumption of complete stationarity. No doubt, as data banks of security prices become available, this form of updating procedure will be practiced in any event. However, for most of the portfolios we wish to consider, the use of a model with updated values of b_j was not feasible with the security price data available at the time the research was conducted.

Sample Data

The sample consists of portfolios of twenty mutual funds over the period 1960 to 1970. The object of the research was to compute B_t for a series of mutual fund portfolios with varying investment objectives under a variety of market conditions. The names of the funds, together with data relating to asset size and investment objective are included in Table 6-1.

Table 6-2 shows the sample funds cross tabulated by size and objective.

While the number of mutual funds from which the sample could have been chosen is extremely large, the feasible set is made a good deal smaller by data

---

[1] Marshall Blume, "Portfolio Theory: A Step Toward Its Practical Application," *Journal of Business* XLIII, no. 2 (April 1970): 152–173.

[2] See, for example, Jack L. Treynor, William W. Priest, Jr., Lawrence Fisher, and Catherine A. Higgins, "Using Portfolio Composition to Estimate Risk," *Financial Analysts Journal* XXIV (September–October 1968): 93–100. Here the authors used an exponential smoothing technique with arbitrarily assigned weights to update values of security b_j.

Table 6-1
Mutual Fund Sample

Number	Investment Company	Year Organized	Assets ($ million) 12/31/59	Assets ($ million) 12/31/68	Portfolio[a] Objective
1	American Investors Fund	1957	3.9	342.0	A
2	Axe Houghton Stock Fund	1932	7.9	94.5	A
3	Broad Street Investing Corp.	1929	165.5	447.1	D
4	Channing Growth Fund	1939	96.9	374.0	A
5	Chemical Fund, Inc.	1938	266.0	547.9	B
6	Colonial Growth Shares, Inc.	1949	67.9	88.7	B
7	Delaware Fund, Inc.	1937	91.1	500.1	A
8	Dreyfus Fund, Inc.	1947	95.1	2,666.4	A
9	Fidelity Fund, Inc.	1930	403.8	894.2	C
10	Fidelity Trend Fund, Inc.	1957	0.5	1,347.2	A
11	Fundamental Investors, Inc.	1932	599.4	1,391.1	C
12	Johnston Mutual Fund, Inc.	1947	11.5	123.7	B
13	Manhattan Fund, Inc.	1966	–	380.0	A
14	Massachusetts Investors Trust	1924	1,557.7	2,292.9	C
15	National Investors Corporation	1937	134.3	795.6	B
16	Oppenheimer Fund, Inc.	1958	4.2	262.7	A
17	Penn Square Mutual Fund	1958	9.4	168.9	A
18	T. Rowe Price Growth Stock Fund Inc.	1950	28.5	514.1	B
19	Putnam Investors Fund, Inc.[b]	1925	335.2	318.1	C
20	Stein Rowe & Farnum Stock Fund Inc.	1958	11.7	114.3	C

[a] A = *maximum capital gain* (volatility: generally high).
B = *long-term growth of capital and income* (volatility: moderately above average).
C = *growth and current income* (volatility: average).
D = *growth and current income with relative stability* (volatility: below average).
These categories are identical to Wiesenberger's categories 1B–1, 1B–2, 11–A, and 11–B. Wiesenberger's categories were not used because eight of the sample investment companies were identified in the *1968 Investment Companies* as part of category 1–A, Large Growth Funds, because of portfolio size alone, regardless of portfolio objective. The written objectives of these eight were examined and each was assigned to its appropriate category. The remaining funds are in the categories assigned by Wiesenberger's *Investment Companies 1968*.
[b] Incorporated Investors, prior to April 1966.

Table 6-2
Sample of Twenty Mutual Funds by Size and Category

Portfolio Objective	Size ($ million)[a]					
	<$100	100–250	250–500	500–1000	>1000	Total
A[b]	2	3	2	1	1	9
B	2		3			5
C	1		1	2	1	5
D	—	—	1	—	—	1
Total	5	3	7	3	2	20

[a]Mean size based on total net assets of 12/31/59 and 12/31/68.
[b]Objective from Table 6–1.

availability considerations.[3] Sources of ten-year-old mutual-fund portfolios are limited. The sources considered were *Moody's Bank and Finance Manuals; Corporate Records Division,* Baker Library, Harvard University Graduate School of Business (where there is an extensive file of Investment Company Reports); Arthur Wiesenberger *Investment Companies*; and Vickers Associates. Although all had substantially complete files for year-end portfolios, quarterly portfolio data were not generally available. (Moody's does report quarterly portfolios for some of the larger funds.) For this reason it was decided to limit the choice of mutual funds to the eighty-five whose portfolios are covered by Vickers Associates.[4] These were screened for fund objective. Since we were primarily interested in application of the model to common-stock portfolios, balanced and income funds were screened out. The few funds employing fiscal vs. calendar quarters were also screened out because of the potential data problems they might present and also because they would unnecessarily complicate the presentation of results. The selection of the final twenty funds was to some extent arbitrary, but was primarily influenced by data availability within Vickers and secondarily by our desire to include a range of fund sizes and objectives within the sample.

Our goal was to examine the portfolios of the twenty sample investment companies over the forty quarters commencing with December 31, 1959, and ending with December 31, 1969. For some of the sample funds, however, the Vickers data were not available back through 1959. In these cases the data collected for the funds' portfolios began with the earliest portfolio for which data

---

[3] Arthur Wiesenberger, *Investment Companies* (New York: Arthur Wiesenberger & Co.) reports on 132 funds in 1960 and 392 in 1969.

[4] Vickers Associates, Inc., 48 Elm Street, Huntington, New York. The other sources were used in the few instances where data were not available from the Vickers' archives. The required data, of course, also exist in the SEC archives; time and cost constraints prohibited serious consideration of this source.

were available. Over the time period considered, there were another thirty-five portfolios for a number of the funds for which Vickers data were not available. Most of these portfolios were secured from another source so that the observations for each fund would be continuous over the sample time period. Table 6-3 shows the complete sample of quarterly portfolios by fund. Of the 800 possible portfolios, data were gathered and coded for 587. Only eight portfolios were lacking from the midst of a set for a particular investment company, at this stage.

All of the securities in each of the 587 portfolios were coded, key-punched and verified. Since some 112,000 separate codings were involved, the occurrence of some error was unavoidable. A number of procedures were employed to detect and eliminate at least all possible gross errors:

1.   All coded securities were screened to insure that they were included within the range of possible security code numbers and to insure that the same code number did not appear twice within the same portfolio.
2.   Any coded security whose value comprised more than 5 percent of the total value of common stocks within the portfolio was confirmed.
3.   A check was made to insure that the total value of coded securities did not exceed the product of the fraction of the portfolio invested in common stock and also the total net assets of the portfolio.
4.   A random sample of 20 portfolios was taken after coding and keypunching and verified against the source data. There were 22 errors among 1833 codings, an error rate of approximately 1.2 percent.

Within the 587 portfolios it was anticipated that it would not be possible to account for all of the securities because of the problem of collecting and processing the data required to compute individual b_j values for non-New York Stock Exchange holdings. The scope of the problem, however, was not anticipated. Unfortunately, it was not possible to make this determination until after all portfolios were coded, keypunched, and processed. For 169 of the portfolios, initial coding of New York Stock Exchange securities accounted for less than 70 percent of the total value of common stock within the portfolio. In addition, there proved to be in excess of 1200 non-New York Stock Exchange securities among the sample portfolios. Because of the considerable cost and effort required to obtain and process the price data required to obtain b_j values for these securities, they have not been included in the sample portfolios.

Since the element of portfolio composition is critical to the reliability of our results—more critical certainly than the *number* of sample portfolios, or continuity over time for the portfolios of a particular investment company, or even the makeup of the particular group of portfolios examined— it was decided to further analyze only those portfolios in which we could account for (had data for) at least 75 percent of the value of common stock plus cash and liquid assets of the portfolio: there are 341 such portfolios. Among these, our coded securities

Table 6-3
Detail of Sample Portfolios

Fund \ Year (Quarter 1 2 3 4)	1959	1960	1961	1962	1963	1964	1965	1966	1967	1968	1969
American Investors								XXX	XXXX	XXX	XXX
Axe Houghton Stock Fund									X	XXXX	XXX
Broad Street Investing	X	XXXX	XXXX	XXXX	XXXX	XXXX	XXXX	XXXX	XXXX	XXXX	XXX
Channing Growth Fund			XXXX	XXXX	XXXX	XXX	XXXX	XXXX	XXXX	XXXX	XXX
Chemical Fund	X	XXXX	XXXX	XXXX	XXXX	XXXX	XXXX	XXXX	XXXX	XXXX	XXX
Colonial Growth Shares	X	XXXX	XXXX	XXXX	XXXX	XXXX	XXXX	XXXX	XXXX	XXXX	XX
Delaware Fund	X	XXXX	XXXX	XXXX	XXXX	XXXX	XXXX	XXXX	XXXX	XXX	
Dreyfus Fund	X	XXXX	XXX	XXXX	XXXX	XXXX	XXXX	XXXX	XXXX	XX X	XXX
Fidelity Fund	X	XXXX	XXXX	XXXX	XXXX	XXXX	XXXX	XXXX	XXXX	XX X	X X
Fidelity Trend Fund				XXX	XXXX	XXXX	XXXX	XXXX	XXXX	XXX	
Fundamental Investors	X	XXXX	XXXX	XXXX	XXXX	XXXX	XXXX	XXXX	XXXX	XXXX	XXX
Johnston Mutual Fund					X	XXXX	XXXX	XXXX	XXXX	XXXX	XXX
Manhattan Fund								XXXX	XXXX	XXXX	XXX
Mass Investors Trust	X	XXXX	XXXX	XXXX	XXXX	XXXX	XXXX	XXXX	XXXX	XXXX	XXX
National Investors Corp.	X	XXXX	XXXX	XXXX	XXXX	XXXX	XXXX	XXXX	XXXX	XXXX	XXX
Oppenheimer Fund								X	XX X	XXXX	XX
Penn Square Mutual Fund	X	XXX	XXXX	XXXX	XXXX	XXXX	XX	XXXX	XXXX	XXXX	XXX
T. Rowe Price Growth Stock	X	XXXX	XXXX	XXXX	XXXX	XXXX	XXXX	XXXX	XXXX	XXXX	XXX
Putnam Investors Fund		XXXX	XXXX	XXXX	XXXX	XXXX	XXXX	XXXX	XXXX	XXXX	XXX
Stein Rowe & Farnum Stock					X	XXX	XXXX	XXXX	XXXX	XXXX	XXX

account for an average of 84 percent of portfolio value. These portfolios are boldface in Table 6-3. As it turns out, the excluded portfolios tend to be those for the same investment companies. Thus five mutual funds were eliminated completely from further consideration and the continuity of observations among the remaining fifteen was not severely damaged. Three of the fifteen, in fact, retained their full complement of forty portfolios.

We have therefore chosen to report on fewer portfolios. The results however will be more reliable, and the decision in no way affects the objectives of the research. If there is nonstationarity of portfolio volatility, we would, of course, have more occasion to observe it among 587 portfolios and perhaps the range of values assumed by B_t would be greater. Yet, while it might be slightly more difficult to observe nonstationarity among 341 portfolios, if it is present, the conclusion could hardly be different if the 587 were used. As far as the other objectives of the research are concerned, these could be accomplished to some degree with as few as twenty or forty portfolios of a single investment company.

Even now with an average of 84 percent of individual portfolio securities accounted for, we must consider how the unaccounted-for balance of 16 percent may influence our results. Note that it will seldom be possible to account for 100 percent of the securities within the portfolio of an investment company, since 5 percent of reported holdings are typically classified as "Other." For these unlocated securities we are making the implicit assumption that their values of b_j on balance, are equal to the weighted average portfolio B_t computed for the parent portfolio. In some ways this is not a very good assumption. Since these securities tend to be American Stock Exchange and over-the-counter issues, including special situations and warrants, their systematic risk is no doubt greater than that of the typical portfolio security. To the extent that this is true, observed values of B_t will be understated. There is one offsetting factor, however. The unaccounted-for group of securities also include the common stock of commercial banks and other nonlisted financial institutions. In six of the ten years in the interval 1960–1969 inclusive, the percent change in the Standard and Poor's Index of nine New York City Banks has been less than the similar changes in the Standard & Poor's 500 Composite Index, suggesting that on balance the financial securities will exert an influence counter to that of the American Stock Exchange and over-the-counter issues. Interestingly enough five of the nine banks that are used to construct this index are included among those one hundred unaccounted-for securities that appear most frequently among the sample portfolios.

However, even if the implicit assumption—noted for the unaccounted-for 16 percent—is not true, and observed values of B_t are either overstated or understated, we can tolerate this imperfection if the unaccounted-for securities affect all the portfolios of the same investment company in a consistent manner; for we are primarily interested in possible changes in portfolio volatility.

If the unaccounted-for portion of the portfolio were to influence values of portfolio volatility in an erratic fashion, it would happen either as the result of a planned policy of the portfolio manager or it could happen accidentally. In the former instance, the portfolio manager would have to make it a practice to adjust portfolio volatility chiefly by changing the composition of the unaccounted-for securities. An unlikely policy, since this can be accomplished more readily and at less cost by moving in or out of cash or a riskless asset. Evidence presented in Chapter 7 suggests that this is, in fact, the primary means employed to adjust the volatility of the same portfolios. But further, in order for us to observe a change in portfolio volatility when there is in fact stability, the portfolio manager must shift this relatively small segment of the portfolio counter to any move we may observe. It would seem that it would require a peculiar set of circumstances to cause the manager to shift the volatilities of segments of his portfolio in opposite directions over the same time period. Even more peculiar would be the instance wherein the segments so shifted matched those of our accounted-for and un-accounted-for partition of the portfolio.

In any event the magnitude of the shift required by an average 16 percent of the portfolio to offset the observed change within 84 percent of the portfolio prohibits serious consideration of this possibility. Turnover among the 16 per-cent would have to be nearly 100 percent and occur only among securities at the opposite extremes of the volatility continuum for either planned or accidental negation of any material change observed between values of B_t. And while it is possible that such an event might happen and might result in an observed change in B_t, when none actually occurred, the combination of cir-cumstances and the magnitude of the net change in the volatilities of the accounted-for securities indicate that it is an unlikely event.

Summary

We will use values of portfolio volatility comprised of the weighted vola-tilities of the securities that make up the portfolios. These values will be used to test the stationarity assumption and a single aspect of the portfolio manager's performance. When observing the results presented in the following chapter, our conclusions can be tempered to the degree indicated by the acceptance of one of the following assumptions.

1. That the higher volatilities of AMEX and OTC stocks are somewhat counter-balanced by those of the banks and financial institutions, both of which are omitted from the analysis; and that the average 16 percent of un-accounted-for securities do have volatilities close to that of the parent port-folio. In which case, all figures reported in Chapter 7 will be accepted as substantially correct.

2. That the unaccounted-for securities affect portfolio volatility in a consistent

manner so that, while reported values of portfolio volatility may be either overstated or understated, any observed changes in volatility represent real changes.

3.   That minor changes in portfolio volatility may be observed when no change actually occurs, but major changes must be significant. This is true because it is unlikely that major observed changes in volatility are being offset by equal and opposite changes effected by the unaccounted-for securities.

4.   That an average of 84 percent for that portion of the portfolio accounted-for is too low. Ninety percent should be the cut-off, in which case concern will be centered on just the portfolios of Funds number 40 and 50.

7

Application of the
Risk-Exposure Model
to Mutual-Fund Portfolios

The purpose of this chapter is to report the results obtained when our model was applied to the sample of 341 mutual-fund portfolios for the 1959–1969 decade. We will:

1. report on the stationarity of portfolio systematic risk;
2. report on the methods employed by the managers of the sample investment companies to adjust portfolio volatility;
3. discuss the utility of the model as a measure of one aspect of a manager's performance — viz., the ability to predict general market turns — and examine the performance of the sample mutual-fund portfolios in this respect.

General Findings

Table 7-1 exhibits the summary statistics for values of B_t computed for the sample portfolios. The results are shown by fund; the funds are arranged by portfolio objective.[1] Interestingly enough, the funds as classified by Wiesenberger on the basis of stated objective and volatility, would, with few exceptions have been classified similarly by the model; for median and mean values of B_t do exhibit a general downward movement as objectives change from that of the most volatile A class to that of the least volatile D group.

It would seem fair to say that, relative to each other and relative to the market, the funds do for the most part operate in their declared risk classes. Risk classes, at least as interpreted and assigned by Wiesenberger, do have meaning for the investor. Those investment companies classified as having a "generally high" volatility do in fact deal in securities with high volatilities. Conversely, for those funds where assigned volatilities are considered average or moderately above average, portfolio managers appear to weight investments in individual securities so as to achieve a portfolio volatility near that of the market volatility.

Portfolio volatility is not stationary for these mutual funds over the time period considered. Spreads between minimum and maximum values range from 7 points to 48 points (relative to a market volatility of 100 points) among the

---

[1] Two portfolios of the Penn Square Mutual Fund are included because at least 75 percent of their portfolio value was accounted for in computing B_t in accordance with the procedure described in Chapter 6. Summary statistics are not presented for these two observations.

Table 7-1
Summary Statistics For B_t by Mutual Fund

Number	Name	Fund Objective[a]	Number of Sample Portfolios	B_t					
				Range		Spread	Mean	SD	Median
				Low	High				
12	Channing Growth Fund	A	13	1.10	1.32	.22	1.22	0.08	1.23
20	Delaware Fund	A	23	0.79	1.27	.48	1.10	0.13	1.11
28	Dreyfus Fund	A	32	0.89	1.15	.26	1.06	0.07	1.07
38	Fidelity Trend Fund	A	17	0.98	1.34	.36	1.24	0.10	1.27
46	Manhattan Fund	A	5	1.11	1.37	.26	1.20	0.10	1.18
60	Penn Square Mutual Fund	A	2	1.04	1.11	–	–	–	–
14	Chemical Fund	B	15	1.05	1.12	.07	1.09	0.02	1.09
44	Johnston Fund	B	16	0.97	1.12	.15	1.04	0.05	1.06
54	National Investors Corp.	B	13	1.07	1.15	.08	1.11	0.02	1.11
64	T. Rowe Price Growth Stock	B	30	0.93	1.12	.19	1.01	0.05	1.01
36	Fidelity Fund	C	33	0.86	1.18	.32	1.04	0.07	1.06
40	Fundamental Investors	C	40	0.92	1.14	.22	1.04	0.06	1.04
50	Mass. Investors Trust	C	40	0.98	1.13	.15	1.01	0.03	1.01
66	Putnam Investors	C	22	0.98	1.25	.27	1.06	0.07	1.04
10	Broad Street Investing	D	40	0.94	1.05	.11	0.98	0.02	0.97
	Total		341						

[a] A = maximum capital gain (Volatility: generally high)
B = long-term growth of capital and income (Volatility: moderately above average)
C = growth and current income (Volatility: average)
D = growth and current income with relative stability (Volatility: below average)

sample funds. The median spread is 22 points. Percent differences between minimum and maximum values of B_t for individual funds range from highs of 61 percent for the Delaware Fund and 37 percent for the two Fidelity Funds to lows of 7 percent for both the Chemical Fund and National Investors Corporation. The remaining ten funds uniformly fill the continuum between these extremes and have an average (median) maximum value that is 22 percent higher than the related minimum. The same variability can be observed in an examination of the standard deviations computed for B_t for each fund.

We also observe that the more risky Class A funds exhibit more volatile volatilities. Measures of both spread and standard deviation are higher for these funds than for those in the other three classes. There does not appear to be a pattern established by objective however, because the magnitudes of volatility spreads are higher for Class C funds than for Class B funds. Given the limited number of sample funds and the small differences among B_t values for sample funds in Classes B and C, it is unlikely that meaningful differences would be observed. It is true, however, that the very nature of the more volatile funds allows them more opportunity to alter their risk exposure significantly, simply because the range of volatilities available to them is greater.

Implications

The finding of nonstationarity has a number of implications for the investor. He can no longer accept measures of ex-post average volatility as sufficient criteria for assessing risk. Two mutual funds, which on the average (over some time interval, e.g., ten years) maintain the same level of volatility, may be two very different investments and will require two different sets of decision criteria. If Fund 1 maintains a stable volatility, in line with a policy of not trying to outguess the market, expectations about future risk can reasonably be based on historical data and assessments can be made of future return given expectations about market return. Neither horizon time nor timing is critical in selecting this fund from among other funds of similar stable volatilities. On the other hand, if a second fund exhibits an unstable or nonstationary volatility, in accordance with a policy to "manage" the portfolio in anticipation of market swings, the opportunities for reward and loss to the investor are much greater than those in Fund 1. And, if the manager is successful in correctly adjusting the volatility of his portfolio to higher than average levels, the rewards on the upside (while consistent with the new level of systematic risk) will be greater than those for Fund 1. Conversely, losses will be less, if the correct adjustment is made to a lower than average volatility prior to a market downturn. The returns adjusted to some average level of systematic risk will be greater for Fund 2 than for Fund 1. If, however, the manager incorrectly adjusts the portfolio volatility, the potential loss is greater for Fund 2. The amount of additional gain or loss depends on the degree of the shift in volatility from its normal level, how far the manager backs his bet on the next market turn, the frequency with which the market makes significant changes in direction, and the magnitude of the swing. A manager who does an average job and calls the turn 50 percent of the time may still provide superior or inferior results for the mean level of portfolio systematic risk maintained, depending on the combinations of (1) the magnitude of shifts in volatility and (2) the size of market turn.

The mutual funds with unstable volatilities can present very different risk dimensions to the investor, conditional on his horizon time. They may also provide opportunities for new investment strategies for what we shall call the "sophisticated investor." Investors with a long-term horizon, e.g., ten years, can expect on average a volatility consistent with the fund's objective and stated risk class. To investors with an intermediate term horizon, the concept of risk class, by itself, may be meaningless. This would be true in any instance where horizon time is not of sufficient length to include at least one full market cycle together with appropriate response in portfolio volatility. For these investors, risk class — as measured by portfolio volatility — is conditioned on the manager's market expectations and may or may not be consistent with the purported risk class of the fund or the volatility expected by the investor.

The investor with a short-term horizon time knows for certain the risk class of all funds under consideration. For it is simply B_t.

If we define a sophisticated investor as one who is willing to form his own market expectations, we can consider an investment strategy based on the selection of investment companies whose current value of B_t is consistent with these expectations. This, of course, also implies a short-term horizon time as defined above and a willingness on the part of the investor to disinvest when observed values of B_t are not in line with his expectations. Note that at any point in time this strategy would include consideration of all investment companies and not just those with unstable volatilities. Transaction costs, which might normally preclude such a strategy, can be eliminated if the investment companies considered are limited to the "no-load" class of mutual funds.[2]

The finding of nonstationarity also has implications for existing measures of portfolio performance. The measures used by both Treynor and Jensen assume stationarity or substantial stationarity of portfolio systematic risk over a ten-year interval.[3] Returns that are superior to those expected for this level of systematic risk are attributed to the manager's ability to identify and deal in securities that are misvalued by the market. Inferior returns are achieved to the extent that the expense of identifying such securities is greater than the return realized on them.

---

[2] Arthur Wiesenberger, *Investment Companies 1969*, reports on sixty-eight of these funds.

[3] Jack L. Treynor, "How to Rate Management of Investment Funds," *Harvard Business Review* XLIII (January–February 1965): 63–75; Michael C. Jensen, "The Performance of Mutual Funds in the Period 1945–1964," *Journal of Finance* XXIII, no. 2 (May 1968): 389–419.

Since portfolio volatility is assumed constant, no consideration is given to superior or inferior returns resulting from the manager's ability to forecast market turns. Presuming that a procedure based on ten annual returns is sufficiently accurate to determine average ex-post portfolio volatility, the results reported by these models are correct for those funds with substantially stationary volatilities. Although there are certain cases in which nonstationary volatility will lead to a biased measure of excess return, these results are also correct in a gross sense for funds which exhibit unstable volatilities. However, in the latter case, superior or inferior risk-adjusted returns cannot be attributed solely to ability to select individual securities. The gross effect is due to both this ability and to the ability to adjust portfolio volatility properly in anticipation of market turns. The measures of performance reported here are more precise to the extent that they allow these different aspects of a manager's performance to be netted out and viewed separately. Conclusions drawn on the basis of the former measures are appropriate only over periods for which volatility does remain constant.

It seems clear that performance broken down in this manner can have very meaningful implications for the division of responsibilities among those concerned with the management of the portfolio and for the allocation of the research budget between these two tasks. Investment companies that are superior in one of these aspects of portfolio management may wish to increase resource expenditures to become more proficient in the other. If these two factors can be isolated, it may also make sense to divide the immediate responsibility for the portfolio between two managers, each a specialist in one element of performance.

Adjusting Portfolio Volatility

In isolating this one aspect of performance we can more fully perceive its significance to the management of the portfolio if we examine the methods used by the manager to effect shifts in volatility and if we can determine the frequency and magnitude of volatility changes. A portfolio manager can adjust volatility in two ways. He can change the composition of the portfolio by moving on balance into more or less volatile securities. He can also increase or decrease his holdings of cash and other riskless assets.[4] And, of course, he may accomplish the change using a combination of these methods. All mutual funds have a full downward mobility in the sense that they can move down from an existing volatility level to any lower level including zero volatility, if fully invested in the riskless asset. Upward mobility, however, is limited for most investment companies. Almost all of the traditional mutual funds are restricted from borrowing.[5]

---

[4] For purposes of this study, portfolio holdings of cash and government securities were considered together as riskless assets.

[5] The newer leverage and hedge funds are not so restricted, nor are some of the older closed-end investment trusts.

These funds can increase portfolio volatility by reducing holdings in the riskless asset but once some minimum transaction or liquidity balance is reached, future increases in volatility can be achieved only by moving into more volatile securities. Opportunities to increase systematic risk using leverage cannot be considered.

The advantage of moving in and out of a riskless asset to adjust volatility is principally the speed with which the adjustment can take place. This occurs because a portion of the portfolio with some volatility is moved into an asset with zero volatility. Transaction costs are reduced since a change in a smaller portion of the portfolio is required to achieve a given volatility change and since the transaction is essentially oneway. Volatility changes accomplished by shifts in portfolio composition, while slower and requiring a turnover of a larger portion of the portfolio, have the advantage of always keeping the fund "fully invested." The portfolio then, in the instance of an unexpected reversal of the market in an upward direction will not be left completely behind the market.

In order to examine the tactics used by the managers of the sample portfolios, values of B_t were computed both gross and net of cash.[6] The measure which includes cash is the B_t for the entire portfolio and the B_t we have referred to until this point. A measure, net of cash, "B_t net," is simply a measure of the volatility of all the common stock within the portfolio. Shifts in "B_t net" with no accompanying change in the portion of the total portfolio invested in cash would indicate that any shift in B_t was caused solely by a change in portfolio composition. On the other hand, changes in B_t with no accompanying change in "B_t net," indicate a shift in volatility caused by a change in the fraction of the portfolio invested in cash.

It is very important to recognize here that some changes in B_t and "B_t net" will occur automatically in response to overall market moves if the portfolio manager does not take any action. Consider the following example of a two-security unmanaged portfolio.

Security	Fraction of Portfolio	b_j	Weighted b_j
A	30%	0.70	0.21
B	60%	1.20	0.72
Cash	10%	0	0

$B_t = 0.93$ "B_t net" = 1.03

If the market moves 20 percent, although values of b_j may remain unchanged, the relative weights applied to the components of the portfolio shift automatically, resulting in changes in both B_t and "B_t net." The new portfolio, assuming a downward market of 20 percent, would appear as follows:

---

[6]The term "cash" will be used in place of the more lengthy "cash and government securities."

Security	Fraction of Portfolio	b_j	Weighted b_j
A	25.8%	0.70	0.181
B	45.6%	1.20	0.547
Cash	28.6%	0	0

$B_t = 0.728$ "B_t net" = 1.02

Of course this occurs because the more volatile securities will decrease more in value in a market downturn than will the less volatile securities or cash, thereby affecting the relative weighting of all components of the portfolio.

It is equally important to note that this automatic change in portfolio volatility for *unmanaged* portfolios need not occur in *managed* portfolios, for the portfolio manager can effect changes in either portfolio composition or weighting to offset undesired changes in portfolio risk exposure. Presumably this is a *raison d'être* for the portfolio manager.

It may be argued that this is true only if the liquidity needs of the portfolio are not changing at the same time. For example, if in the situation described above, an increase in the proportion of cash held were necessary to prepare for an expected increase in redemptions, the manager's ability to readjust portfolio volatility to some desired level would be impaired. Research conducted to date however, suggests just the opposite in this situation.[7] Mutual-fund redemptions tend to fall off in bear markets and increase in new bull markets. So that the need for liquidity may even be less in this example, thus providing the portfolio manager with even more flexibility in adjusting the level of risk exposure.

Since we are dealing with managed portfolios in all cases, in the discussion that follows we shall assume that the observed portfolio volatility is representative of the volatility desired by the portfolio manager.

Table 7-2 presents the data for some of the major quarter-to-quarter shifts in portfolio volatility. Of the 341 sample portfolios it was possible to compute quarterly percent change in B_t for 310. These 310 were divided into two groupings, those with interquarter changes in B_t greater than plus or minus 5 percent and those with changes less than 5 percent. There were fifty-four portfolios that showed quarterly changes in B_t greater than 5 percent. The portfolios and percent changes are shown chronologically by fund in Table 7-2. This table also reports values of "B_t net" and percent of portfolio invested in cash for both the quarter in question and the immediately preceding quarter.

In general, portfolio volatility net of cash is more stable than the portion of the portfolio invested in cash — the latter portion fluctuates widely and appears to account for most of the change observed in B_t. Although the median quarterly percent change in B_t is 7¼ percent, in only fourteen instances is the change in

---

[7] Frank B. Campanella, "An Investigation of the Economic and Financial Variables That Influence Mutual Fund Industry Sales and Redemptions," unpublished paper for the Investment Company Institute, 1970.

Table 7–2
Quarterly Change in B_t by Fund (for changes in excess of 5%)

Fund	Year	Quarter t	B_t Percent Change	"B_t net" t – 1	"B_t net" t	"B_t net" Percent Change	Percent Cash t – 1	Percent Cash t
10	1967	4	7.2	1.05	1.06	0.7	6.8	0.8
12	1964	3	-7.7	1.33	1.28	-3.4	4.5	8.7
	1965	1	10.2	1.26	1.33	5.4	5.5	1.2
	1966	1	-5.6	1.36	1.33	-2.2	4.4	7.7
	1966	3	-8.0	1.34	1.31	-2.9	11.2	15.8
	1967	3	16.4	1.25	1.34	7.4	10.4	2.9
20	1960	2	-6.3	1.11	1.10	-1.0	4.4	9.6
	1965	4	5.9	1.25	1.28	2.4	4.5	1.2
	1966	3	-27.6	1.33	1.29	-2.6	8.4	31.9
	1968	1	-8.6	1.16	1.15	-0.5	25.3	31.4
28	1960	3	-12.8	1.19	1.14	-4.8	7.8	15.6
	1961	4	-7.5	1.06	1.05	-1.7	9.7	15.0
	1962	2	9.8	1.04	1.05	1.1	12.5	4.9
	1964	1	7.2	1.12	1.20	7.1	4.3	4.2
	1966	3	-8.3	1.22	1.20	-1.4	8.0	14.4
	1966	4	6.0	1.20	1.20	-0.1	14.4	9.1
	1967	4	-5.5	1.17	1.16	-1.5	3.9	7.8
	1968	1	-6.6	1.16	1.14	-1.0	7.8	13.0
36	1960	1	-14.0	1.13	1.09	-4.0	7.0	16.7
	1960	3	6.3	1.08	1.08	0.6	19.0	14.4
	1960	4	7.3	1.08	1.09	0.7	14.4	8.8
	1961	1	9.4	1.09	1.10	1.2	8.8	1.4
	1962	2	-13.0	1.09	1.07	-1.9	2.5	13.5
	1962	3	-6.8	1.07	1.06	-1.1	13.5	18.5
	1962	4	9.2	1.06	1.04	-2.0	18.5	9.1
	1963	1	9.4	1.04	1.05	1.3	9.1	1.8
	1964	1	9.5	1.08	1.12	3.5	6.7	1.3
	1965	4	5.5	1.15	1.20	4.2	2.5	1.2
	1966	1	-8.8	1.20	1.20	0.5	1.2	10.4
	1966	3	-5.0	1.20	1.15	-4.5	11.8	12.3
	1967	1	5.7	1.15	1.13	-1.6	10.9	4.3
38	1965	1	5.1	1.31	1.35	3.3	2.8	1.1
	1966	2	-7.2	1.41	1.41	0.1	9.6	16.2
	1966	3	-5.6	1.41	1.38	-1.8	16.2	19.4
	1967	1	10.6	1.35	1.35	0.0	15.7	6.7
	1967	4	-11.1	1.32	1.27	-3.2	5.0	12.7
40	1966	1	5.6	1.10	1.16	5.1	2.8	2.3
	1966	3	-8.7	1.18	1.17	-1.0	4.0	11.5
	1968	1	-6.8	1.17	1.16	-1.4	2.7	8.1
46	1966	2	-5.9	1.39	1.35	-3.1	15.0	17.4
	1966	3	6.4	1.35	1.40	3.9	17.4	15.4
	1967	1	16.8	1.36	1.43	5.1	14.0	4.4
50	1967	4	6.6	1.06	1.07	1.0	3.0	-2.4
	1968	4	7.3	1.07	1.08	1.6	1.6	-3.9
	1969	1	-7.8	1.08	1.07	-1.0	-3.9	3.2
60	1965	4	6.9	1.19	1.21	1.8	12.5	8.1

Table 7–2, cont.

Fund	Year	Quarter t	Percent B_t Change	"B_t net" $t-1$	"B_t net" t	Percent Change	Percent Cash $t-1$	Percent Cash t
64	1961	3	7.3	1.08	1.09	0.5	13.6	7.8
	1962	3	−6.1	1.08	1.05	−2.5	5.5	9.0
	1963	2	5.4	1.08	1.10	2.1	9.1	6.2
	1965	1	−5.3	1.14	1.11	−2.2	5.8	8.8
	1966	3	7.4	1.16	1.14	−1.5	17.9	10.5
66	1965	4	5.5	1.08	1.10	1.9	8.8	5.6
	1966	3	−8.1	1.14	1.11	−2.3	4.7	10.3
	1968	1	−6.9	1.15	1.15	−0.7	8.4	14.1

B_t accompanied by a change in "B_t net" greater than 3 percent. In all but six cases the change in both "B_t net" and cash is consistent with the change in B_t. That is, an increase in B_t is accompanied by an increase in "B_t net" and a decrease in the fraction of the portfolio held in cash; and, conversely, a decrease in B_t is accompanied by a decrease in "B_t net" and an increase in cash. In these six instances "B_t net" moves counter to the direction expected. In all six instances the percent change in B_t, however, is not greater than 2 percent.

If the fraction of the portfolio invested in cash were to remain constant between two successive quarters, at the level of either quarter, any percent change in "B_t net" would be accompanied by an identical change in B_t. The extent to which these differ is, then, a direct measure of the relative effect of changes in cash holdings and shifts in portfolio composition on portfolio volatility. For the fifty-four portfolios under consideration, if the fraction invested in cash were assumed constant between pairs of successive quarters, on the average (median), one fourth of the change in B_t is accounted for by changes in portfolio composition. The remaining three-fourths is caused by changes in the cash account.

Perhaps a final way to view the impact of cash as a tool to effect changes in portfolio volatility is to examine the relative variability of B_t and "B_t net." From Table 7–2, percent changes in the former run from −28% to +17%, while similarly measured changes in the latter are limited to −4.2% to +7.2%. The same effect can be observed if we compare the range and standard deviation of B_t and "B_t net" for the full sample of 341 portfolios. This comparison is shown by investment company in Table 7–3.

In only one instance, Fund 44, is the range of "B_t net" greater than that of B_t. Standard deviations of "B_t net" exceed those of B_t in only three cases. In each case, however, the difference is small. Note that the range of B_t for each fund is limited on the upside by the maximum value of "B_t net." Only in the case where a fund is allowed to borrow would we expect to find examples where B_t exceeded the highest value of "B_t net." Table 7–3 does show one example of this kind. In the case of Fund 50, B_t is 1.13 while "B_t net" is 1.09. This occurs

Table 7-3
Relative Variability of Portfolio Volatility and Portfolio Volatility Net
of Cash

Fund Number	B_t				"B_t net"			
	Range				Range			
	Low	High	Spread	SD	Low	High	Spread	SD
12	1.10	1.32	.22	.08	1.25	1.36	.11	.03
20	0.79	1.27	.48	.13	1.07	1.33	.26	.08
28	0.89	1.15	.26	.07	1.03	1.22	.19	.05
38	0.98	1.34	.36	.10	1.27	1.41	.14	.04
46	1.11	1.37	.26	.10	1.35	1.43	.08	.03
60	1.04	1.11	–	–	1.19	1.21	–	–
14	1.05	1.12	.07	.02	1.09	1.14	.05	.01
44	0.97	1.12	.15	.05	1.02	1.18	.16	.06
54	1.07	1.15	.08	.02	1.10	1.16	.06	.02
64	0.93	1.12	.19	.05	1.05	1.19	.14	.03
36	0.86	1.18	.32	.07	1.04	1.20	.16	.04
40	0.92	1.14	.22	.06	0.97	1.18	.21	.07
50	0.98	1.13	.15	.03	0.99	1.09	.10	.03
66	0.98	1.25	.27	.07	1.08	1.32	.24	.06
10	0.94	1.05	.11	.02	0.95	1.06	.11	.03

because the Vickers records list two of the portfolios of this fund with small
negative fractions of the portfolio in cash. These were interpreted as borrowings
by our model. Note also that, on the downside, minimum values of B_t are quite a
bit lower than minimum values of "B_t net." And that it is this difference that
accounts for most of the observed differences in spreads between gross and net
value of B_t. This again just reflects the fact that investment managers have more
freedom in adjusting portfolio volatility when the desired move is in a downward
direction.

Volatility and Performance Measurement

For the typical mutual-fund investor as well as for many of those responsible
for pension funds and trusts, one of the prime reasons for placing the investment
in the hands of a fund or investment advisor is to attain professional management.
Selection of a particular mutual fund is usually based on some notion of relative
riskiness and management ability. Assessments of management ability, for investment companies where volatility is unstable, must be sensitive to the degree of
managerial success obtained in the adjustment of B_t. For these investors then,
some measure of success or failure in adjusting volatility in anticipation of market
moves is essential. In this final section we would like to present such a measure.

The standard we propose is a specific measure of ex-post performance. Unfortunately, one of the few criteria available for judging the quality of management is past performance. And the phrase "track record" is certainly not unfamiliar to the investment community. The measure of performance presented is simply an attempt to isolate and measure one element of a manager's track record.

We discussed earlier the notion that portfolio managers who are able to forecast market movements should adjust portfolio volatility in anticipation of such movements. We have found, in fact, that considerable adjustment in volatility does take place.

Although there is a built-in mechanism that tends to reduce portfolio volatility in market downturns and increase it in market upturns, we are clearly working with a sample of *managed* portfolios. Risk exposure can be adjusted and readjusted at the managers' discretion. The performance measure proposed simply relates these adjustments to market movements. We shall assume that the mean ex-post portfolio volatility over the interval for which we have data is the normal level of risk exposure desired by the fund. Given the high correlation between rankings of funds by this standard and by Wiesenberger objective, this would appear to be a reasonable assumption.[8] Actually a modal volatility prior to and during periods of market stability would be a superior choice. Given the data constraints and the nature of the market over the decade under consideration, it is not possible to use such a value here.

For each fund, quarterly portfolio volatility was plotted together with the quarterly levels of the Standard & Poor's 500 Composite Index. Two typical diagrams are shown here as Figure 7-1 and Figure 7-2. Similar diagrams for the remaining mutual funds may be found in the appendix.[9] Figure 7-1 depicts the levels of portfolio volatility for Fund 28. The broken horizontal line across the center of the page locates the mean value of B_t for the company. If a fund is successful in adjusting portfolio volatility in anticipation of market movements, plotted volatilities should appear as a leading series in this figure, since an anticipated market downturn would be preceded by a decrease in volatility and an anticipated market upturn would be preceded by an increase in portfolio volatility. An examination of these two figures as well as those in the appendix clearly shows that this is not the case. In almost all instances, plotted values of B_t are concurrent with or lag plotted levels of the market index. Fund 28 was selected because it has one of the better records in this regard. It moved to a classic minimum value of B_t just prior to the 28 percent downward move in the market index in the first half of 1962. It adjusted volatility downward (but not below the mean level) prior to the 22 percent fall in the market during the first

---

[8]It will be seen that this assumption is critical to just one aspect of the findings presented.

[9]To preserve the continuity of the B_t line, in some cases portfolios were plotted where the fraction of accounted-for securities fell between 70 percent and 75 percent. These portfolios are indicated by breaks in the B_t line both here and in the appendix.

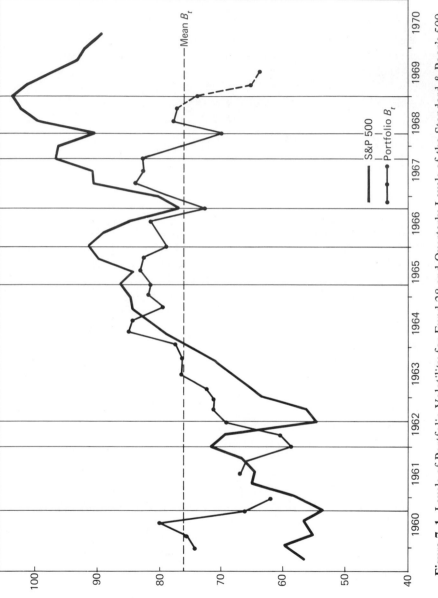

Figure 7-1. Levels of Portfolio Volatility for Fund 28 and Quarterly Levels of the Standard & Poor's 500 Composite Index

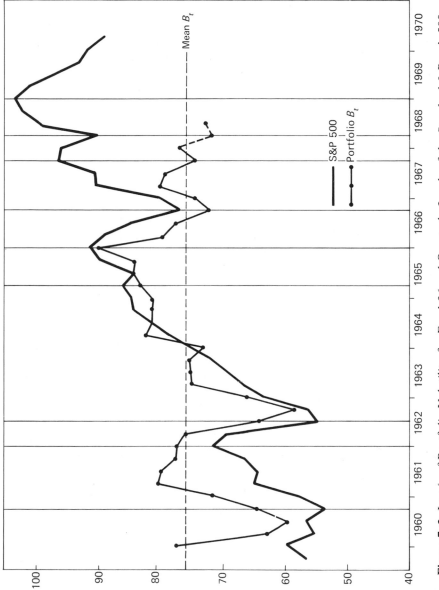

Figure 7–2. Levels of Portfolio Volatility for Fund 36 and Quarterly Levels of the Standard & Poor's 500 Composite Index

three quarters of 1966. However, it reversed this adjustment in the first two quarters of 1966 and then moved to a new low level of B_t just as the market bottomed out, whereupon it moved to a near high just prior to the 1967–1968 downturn, and subsequently moved to a new low volatility again as the market bottomed out. Fund 36 in Figure 7–2 showed some ability to adjust volatility in 1961, but in most cases its volatility peaked just before market downturns and bottomed out prior to market upturns. Most of the sample funds exhibit this unfortunate characteristic.

To summarize these movements quantitatively, we counted the number of times the portfolio volatility was above and below its average value prior to market upturns and also prior to market downturns. The results are shown in Table 7–4. Of the 339 portfolios[10] for which B_t was computed, 221 occurred prior to market upturns. In only 94 of these 221 instances were values of B_t above their average level. Only five of the fourteen funds exhibited above average volatility more frequently than below average volatility prior to a positive market move. Similarly there were 118 observations prior to negative market movements. In only 38 of these instances were the portfolio volatilities below their average level for each mutual fund. There were just two funds, where B_t was below average more frequently than above average, prior to these downward market moves.

A second more direct test of managers' predictive ability was also made. Portfolio volatility was recorded solely at market peaks and troughs. Table 7–5 identifies the point in time when four definite troughs and four definite peaks occur. The volatility of each fund's portfolios for which observations were available are recorded at these times.

Of the 339 portfolios, 67 appear at either a peak or a trough; 36 at troughs and 31 at peaks. Of the 36 observations of B_t appearing at market bottoms, only eight were above the average level for the fund in question. Among the 31 observations of B_t at market peaks just 5 were below values of fund mean B_t.

The results presented in Table 7–4 are quite sensitive to the mean level of B_t for the few funds with relatively stable volatilities. Note for example, the effect of shifting the mean B_t line for Fund 10, which has quite a stable volatility over a five-year interval. Table 7–5 is also based on comparisons with a standard defined as mean B_t; and while changes in mean B_t would not affect the results for funds with unstable volatilities, minor shifts, in some cases of stable volatility, would influence the results. Of course, it might be argued, in these latter instances the fund manager while not being a perverse predictor is not a good predictor, for in Table 7–5 we are referring to market peaks and bottoms and in most cases substantial market changes. In these cases we would not on balance expect the portfolios of managers with predictive ability to be hovering about an average level of B_t. Rather we would expect well-below average volatilities at peaks and above average volatilities at troughs.

---

[10]The two portfolios for Fund 60 were not included.

Table 7-4
Volatility Levels for Quarter t Related to Market Movements in Quarter $t + 1$

			Portfolio Volatility					
			Market Up			Market Down		
Fund	Portfolios	Fund Objective	Above Average	Below Average	Average	Above Average	Below Average	Average
12	13	A	3	5	0	4	1	0
20	23	A	9[a]	7	0	4	3	0
28	32	A	12[a]	10	0	7	3	0
38	17	A	8[a]	3	0	5	1	0
46	5	A	1	2	0	0	2[a]	0
14	15	B	3	6	1	2	1	2
44	16	B	5	6	0	4	1	0
54	13	B	5[a]	3	0	3	1	1
64	30	B	11[a]	8	1	3	7[a]	0
36	33	C	10	12	0	9	2	0
40	40	C	9	16	0	10	5	0
50	40	C	8	16	1	12	3	0
66	22	C	3	10	2	4	3	0
10	40	D	7	17	1	7	5	3
Subtotal	339		94	121	6	74	38	6
Total	339		221			118		

[a]Portfolios in correct volatility position for more than 50 percent of the observations.

Table 7-5
Portfolio Volatility Prior to Major Market Turns

Fund	Objective	Mean Volatility	Market Bottom				Market Peak			
			Yr Qtr 60 3	Yr Qtr 62 2	Yr Qtr 66 3	Yr Qtr 68 1	Yr Qtr 61 4	Yr Qtr 65 4	Yr Qtr 67 3	Yr Qtr 68 4
12	A	1.22	—	—	1.10	—	—	1.30	1.30	—
20	A	1.10	0.98	1.06	0.88	0.79	—	1.26	—	—
28	A	1.06	0.96	0.99	1.03	1.00	0.89[a]	1.09	1.13	—
38	A	1.24	—	0.98	1.11	—	—	1.29	1.25	—
46	A	1.20	—	—	1.18	—	—	—	—	—
14	B	1.09	1.06	1.09	—	—	1.09	—	—	—
44	B	1.04	—	—	1.09[a]	—	—	1.07	1.10	—
54	B	1.11	1.12[a]	1.08	—	—	1.12	—	—	—
64	B	1.01	—	1.02[a]	1.02[a]	—	1.01	1.00[a]	—	—
36	C	1.04	0.93	0.93	1.01	—	1.06	1.18	1.03[a]	—
40	C	1.04	1.02	0.95	1.03	1.06[a]	1.01[a]	1.07	1.12	1.09
50	C	1.01	1.02[a]	0.99	0.98	1.04[a]	1.02	1.02	1.03	1.13
66	C	1.06	—	—	1.00	0.98	1.14	1.04[a]	—	—
10	D	0.98	0.98	0.95	0.97	1.03[a]	1.00	0.97	0.98	0.98

[a]Above average prior to market upturn or below average prior to market downturn.

Table 7-6

Minimum and Maximum Levels of Fund B_t Related to Market Changes in the Following Quarter

Fund	Objective	Min. B_t	Change in Market (percent)	Max. B_t	Change in Market (percent)
12	A	1.10	5.9	1.32	-1.6
20	A	0.79	11.2	1.27	-4.2
28	A	0.89	-2.1[a]	1.15	4.2[a]
38	A	0.98	3.7	1.34	-1.6
46	A	1.11	-8.8[a]	1.37	1.3[a]
14	B	1.05	3.7	1.12	6.3[a]
44	B	0.97	1.4	1.12	13.2[a]
54	B	1.07	13.1	1.15	0.1[a]
64	B	0.93	-6.8[a]	1.12	-5.7
36	C	0.86	13.1	1.18	-2.7
40	C	0.92	13.1	1.14	-5.7
50	C	0.98	5.4	1.13	-1.5
66	C	0.98	3.5	1.25	-6.8
10	D	0.94	13.1	1.05	-5.7

[a]Portfolio volatility at a minimum prior to a downward market move.
Portfolio volatility at a maximum prior to an upward market move.

However, in anticipation of some criticism on this score, one additional test was made of managers' predictive ability. We noted the extreme values of B_t and observed the market action in the following period. Table 7-6 presents these data.

For the fourteen funds, in only three cases were minimum values of B_t followed by market downturns. As a matter of fact, five of these minimum observations preceded upward market movements in excess of 10 percent. Five of the fund maximum levels of B_t were followed by market upturns. The remaining nine occurred prior to market downturns. Here also the data indicate strongly that the fund managers have no ability to predict changes in the market.

Further examination of the plotted values of B_t for each fund suggest an "odd-lot" type theory at work. Managers tend to allow portfolio volatility to increase during rising market periods achieving a maximum value just as the market peaks. Volatility is then allowed to fall during the subsequent down market until the market bottoms out, at which point fund volatility is near a minimum value.

Summary

Applying the risk-exposure model to a sample of 341 mutual portfolios scattered over the 1960 decade, we found that the systematic risk of the fourteen mutual funds examined was not stationary. For some of the funds, in fact, it moved over a substantial range. Mean levels of fund B_t placed the funds in substantially the same risk class as those assigned by Wiesenberger. This implies some element of validity either to our measure or to Wiesenberger's interpretation of the fund's stated objective, depending on how you approach the problem. In any event it is comforting that these independent appraisals of fund risk exposure are consistent, and that mutual funds appear to operate on average within the bounds of their purported objective. We observed and discussed the more unstable volatilities of investment companies at the more risky end of the continuum. We also noted that shifts in portfolio volatility were accomplished more frequently by adjusting the fraction of the portfolio invested in cash than by substantially changing portfolio composition. For some funds at least, this would indicate that observation of the cash account alone may provide a fair proxy for examining a manager's ability to call market movements. Finally, we used our measure of risk exposure to assess the fund manager's ability to adjust the portfolio in anticipation of the next market move. The results for the sample funds over the time period studied suggest extremely limited ability in this area.[11] If the nature of the automatic adjustment in volatility is offered as the reason for the reported result, the equally damaging conclusion of no effective management of risk exposure must be admitted as a corollary.

Future Research

The most obvious need for additional work involves the expansion of this study to include more portfolios for a broader sample of investment companies. The sample employed in this research was limited to a great extent by the task of collecting and coding portfolio composition data and then further collecting and coding price data for a large number of securities. Now that both portfolio composition data and security price data are becoming available in directly processable form, it should not be extremely difficult to duplicate this work with a larger sample size two years hence.

In the text we mentioned the need for more research in the area of measuring the systematic risk of individual securities. Based on the evidence presented herein and elsewhere it seems unlikely that a great number of securities have completely stationary systematic risk elements. The identification of those securities for which this assumption is questionable could greatly reduce the scope of the adjustments required in subsequent research. Again, the growing data banks of daily price data for many securities should facilitate this task.

---

[11] Similar findings both with respect to the nonstationarity of portfolios volatility and the lack of predictive ability on the part of mutual fund portfolio managers were reported by Richard S. Bower and J. Peter Williamson at the annual meeting of the Appalachian Finance Association on April 16, 1971.

In addition, more work must be done in devising and testing versions of the multi-index model. If, as this research indicates, average portions of security variability explained by the market are decreasing over time, the usefulness of the single-index model will be limited. Our surprising relative success with a rather naive multi-index model, based on one-digit industry codes, suggests that this might be a place to commence future study.

Finally, in our assessment of a manager's ability to adjust portfolio composition in anticipation of market movements, we have implicitly assumed that he views security volatility in a manner not significantly different than that specified by our computed value of b_j. While this is not as critical an assumption as it might otherwise be for most investment companies because of the influence of "cash" adjustments on portfolio volatility, it would be of value if an investigation were made of portfolio managers' perceptions of security volatility. A full research project involving interviews with fund managers could accomplish a great deal in this area. Perhaps a rank ordering of securities by perceived volatility could be compared with a similar ordering provided by the model.

In closing, this research has accomplished further empirical testing of the single-index market model. Using this model, it has examined the stationarity over time of the volatilities of managed portfolios. Our research has also proposed and tested an application of the model for the purpose of assessing one aspect of portfolio management and performance.

Appendix A

Distribution of Security b_j and R^2 for Samples
of NYSE Securities for Various Time Periods
and Differencing Intervals

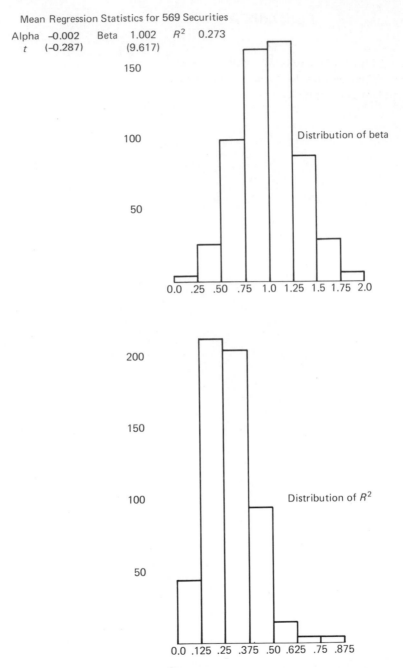

Mean Regression Statistics for 569 Securities

Alpha –0.002   Beta   1.002 R^2 0.273
 t (–0.287)   (9.617)

Distribution of beta

Distribution of R^2

Figure A-1. Beta and R^2 Distributions: Monthly Observations – January 1946 to June 1966.

Mean Regression Statistics for 569 Securities

Alpha   0.000   Beta   0.999 R^2 0.245
  t   (0.096)   (6.325

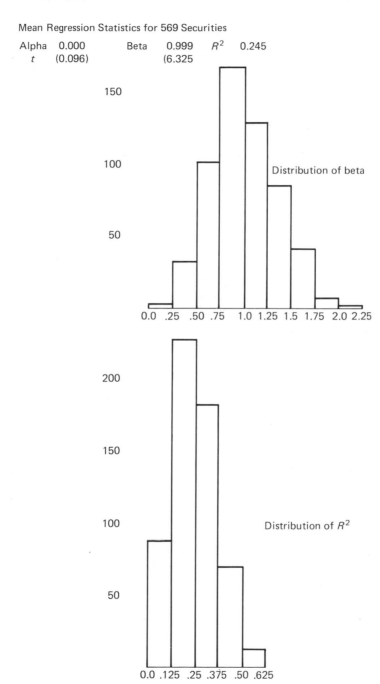

Figure A–2. Beta and R^2 Distributions. Monthly Observations –
January 1956 to June 1966.

Mean Regression Statistics for 569 Securities

Alpha   0.000   Beta   1.112 R^2 0.281
   t (−0.04)   (5.014)

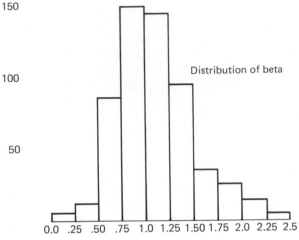

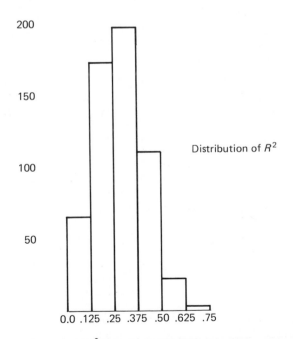

Figure A-3. Beta and R^2 Distributions: Monthly Observations — January 1961 to June 1966.

Mean Regression Statistics for 569 Securities

Alpha   −0.007   Beta   1.077 R^2 0.331
  t (−0.434)   (6.388)

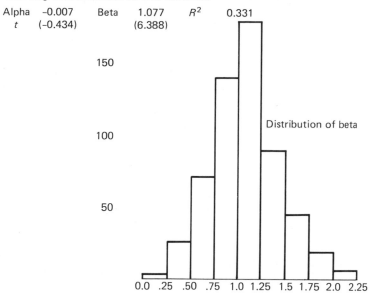

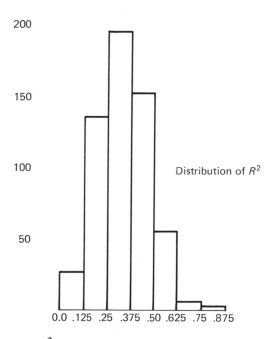

Figure A-4. Beta and R^2 Distributions: Quarterly Observations –
January 1946 to June 1966.

Mean Regression Statistics for 569 Securities

Alpha −0.001   Beta   1.097 R^2 0.401
  t (−0.037)   (3.828)

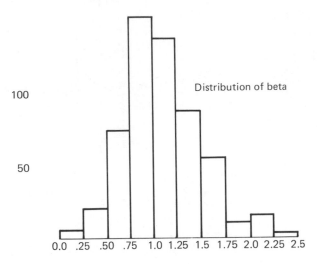

Distribution of beta

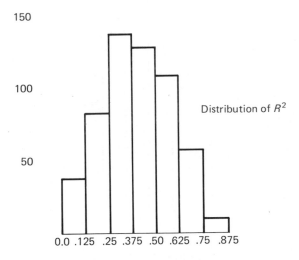

Distribution of R^2

Figure A-5. Beta and R^2 Distributions: Quarterly Observations — January 1961 to June 1966.

Appendix B

**Correlations of Market Model Residuals for a
Sample of 100 NYSE Securities, Identified by
Name and Industry Class**

Table B-1. Market Model. Listing of Companies with Most Highly Correlated Residuals

NO	RMAX	SEC ID		SEC ID		INDUSTRYS	
1	0.7382	1322	SKELLY OIL	1008	MISSION CORP	291	671
2	0.6647	1234	REPUBLIC STEEL CORP	831	JONES & LAUGHLIN STEEL CORP	331	331
3	0.5983	1540	US STEEL	831	JONES & LAUGHLIN STEEL CORP	331	331
4	0.5974	1540	US STEEL	1234	REPUBLIC STEEL CORP	331	331
5	0.5858	1540	US STEEL	195	BETHLEHEM STEEL CORP	331	331
6	0.5701	831	JONES & LAUGHLIN STEEL CORP	195	BETHLEHEM STEEL CORP	331	331
7	0.5456	1540	US STEEL	119	ARMCO STEEL CORP	331	331
8	0.5360	1234	REPUBLIC STEEL CORP	119	ARMCO STEEL CORP	331	331
9	0.5343	661	GOODYEAR TIRE AND RUBBER	572	FIRESTONE TIRE & RUBBER CO	301	301
10	0.5259	1305	SHARON STEEL CORP	831	JONES & LAUGHLIN STEEL CORP	331	331
11	0.5197	1432	TEXACO	1358	STANDARD OIL OF CALIF.	291	291
12	0.5124	831	JONES & LAUGHLIN STEEL CORP	119	ARMCO STEEL CORP	331	331
13	0.5087	1234	REPUBLIC STEEL CORP	195	BETHLEHEM STEEL CORP	331	331
14	0.4805	1322	SKELLY OIL	997	CONTINENTAL OIL	291	291
15	0.4646	1432	TEXACO	1361	STANDARD OIL OF NEW JERSEY	291	291
16	0.4632	793	INTERNATIONAL PAPER	426	CROWN ZELLERBACH CORP	262	262
17	0.4591	1020	MONSANTO CO	487	DOW CHEMICAL CO	281	281
18	0.4553	1305	SHARON STEEL CORP	1234	REPUBLIC STEEL CORP	331	331
19	0.4549	1242	REYNOLDS TOBACCO	1179	PHILIP MORRIS INC	211	211
20	0.4528	1359	STANDARD OIL OF INDIANA	997	CONTINENTAL OIL	291	291
21	0.4439	661	GOODYEAR TIRE AND RUBBER	659	GOODRICH BF	301	301
22	0.4399	1359	STANDARD OIL OF INDIANA	1322	SKELLY OIL	291	291
23	0.4384	1359	STANDARD OIL OF INDIANA	40	AMERADA PETROLEUM CORP	291	131
24	0.4377	1358	STANDARD OIL OF CALIF.	998	GULF OIL CORP	291	291
25	0.4356	1308	SHELL OIL CO	997	CONTINENTAL OIL	291	291
26	0.4284	1322	SKELLY OIL	1308	SHELL OIL CO	291	291
27	0.4245	1361	STANDARD OIL OF NEW JERSEY	1358	STANDARD OIL OF CALIF.	291	291
28	0.4230	831	JONES & LAUGHLIN STEEL CORP	21	ALLEGHENY LUDLUM STEEL	331	331
29	0.4216	1234	REPUBLIC STEEL CORP	21	ALLEGHENY LUDLUM STEEL	331	331
30	0.4207	1305	SHARON STEEL CORP	195	BETHLEHEM STEEL CORP	331	331
31	0.4176	1008	MISSION CORP	997	CONTINENTAL OIL	671	291
32	0.4169	1322	SKELLY OIL	40	AMERADA PETROLEUM CORP	291	131
33	0.4119	1361	STANDARD OIL OF NEW JERSEY	998	GULF OIL CORP	291	291
34	0.4096	1359	STANDARD OIL OF INDIANA	1358	STANDARD OIL OF CALIF.	291	291
35	0.4082	997	CONTINENTAL OIL	40	AMERADA PETROLEUM CORP	291	131
36	0.4081	195	BETHLEHEM STEEL CORP	119	ARMCO STEEL CORP	331	331
37	0.4043	1322	SKELLY OIL	1181	PHILLIPS PETROLEUM	291	291
38	0.4032	1308	SHELL OIL CO	1181	PHILLIPS PETROLEUM	291	291
39	0.4027	1482	UNION CARBIDE CORP	487	DOW CHEMICAL CO	287	281
40	0.4027	1358	STANDARD OIL OF CALIF.	1008	MISSION CORP	291	671
41	0.3962	1181	PHILLIPS PETROLEUM	997	CONTINENTAL OIL	291	291
42	0.3945	1540	US STEEL	1305	SHARON STEEL CORP	331	331
43	0.3940	1432	TEXACO	1008	MISSION CORP	291	671
44	0.3914	1432	TEXACO	998	GULF OIL CORP	291	291
45	0.3892	119	ARMCO STEEL CORP	21	ALLEGHENY LUDLUM STEEL	331	331
46	0.3881	1181	PHILLIPS PETROLEUM	1008	MISSION CORP	291	671
47	0.3850	1359	STANDARD OIL OF INDIANA	1181	PHILLIPS PETROLEUM	291	291
48	0.3833	1536	US RUBBER	661	GOODYEAR TIRE AND RUBBER	301	301
49	0.3798	1358	STANDARD OIL OF CALIF.	997	CONTINENTAL OIL	291	291
50	0.3775	629	GENERAL MOTORS	333	CHRYSLER CORP	371	371

Rank	Coefficient	Code	Company
51	0.3761	1176	PHELPS DODGE
52	0.3738	1358	STANDARD OIL OF CALIF.
53	0.3726	1008	MISSION CORP
54	0.3714	1536	US RUBBER
55	0.3666	785	INTERNATIONAL HARVESTER
56	0.3656	1305	SHARON STEEL CORP
57	0.3628	1361	STANDARD OIL OF NEW JERSEY
58	0.3628	659	GOODRICH BF
59	0.3602	1361	STANDARD OIL OF NEW JERSEY
60	0.3555	1176	PHELPS DODGE
61	0.3539	1359	STANDARD OIL OF INDIANA
62	0.3504	1308	SHELL OIL CO
63	0.3495	1308	SHELL OIL CO
64	0.3490	1432	TEXACO
65	0.3455	1432	TEXACO
66	0.3455	1432	TEXACO
67	0.3391	1361	STANDARD OIL OF NEW JERSEY
68	0.3381	1181	PHILLIPS PETROLEUM
69	0.3363	863	KRESGE SS
70	0.3347	1359	STANDARD OIL OF INDIANA
71	0.3319	1359	STANDARD OIL OF INDIANA
72	0.3306	831	JONES & LAUGHLIN STEEL CORP
73	0.3296	487	DOW CHEMICAL CO
74	0.3269	395	CONTINENTAL CAN CO INC
75	0.3255	1099	NORTHWEST AIRLINES
76	0.3251	1527	UNITED STATES GYPSUM
77	0.3243	1361	STANDARD OIL OF NEW JERSEY
78	0.3217	1361	STANDARD OIL OF NEW JERSEY
79	0.3199	1316	SIMMONS CO
80	0.3171	1482	UNION CARBIDE CORP
81	0.3155	1099	NORTHWEST AIRLINES
82	0.3153	497	DUPONT
83	0.3125	1020	MONSANTO CO
84	0.3119	785	INTERNATIONAL HARVESTER
85	0.3088	1358	STANDARD OIL OF CALIF.
86	0.3075	1176	PHELPS DODGE
87	0.3070	1540	US STEEL
88	0.3061	831	JONES & LAUGHLIN STEEL CORP
89	0.3056	1361	STANDARD OIL OF NEW JERSEY
90	0.3016	1540	US STEEL
91	0.2997	1099	NORTHWEST AIRLINES
92	0.2980	1536	US RUBBER
93	0.2970	998	GULF OIL CORP
94	0.2957	1358	STANDARD OIL OF CALIF.
95	0.2948	1305	SHARON STEEL CORP
96	0.2948	1305	SHARON STEEL CORP
97	0.2944	793	INTERNATIONAL PAPER
98	0.2904	303	CERRO CORP
99	0.2901	195	BETHLEHEM STEEL CORP
100	0.2897	1452	TIMKEN ROLLER BEARING

Code	Company		
848	KENNECOTT COPPER	333	333
1322	SKELLY OIL	291	291
40	AMERADA PETROLEUM CORP	671	131
659	GOODRICH BF	301	301
451	DEERE & CO	352	352
21	ALLEGHENY LUDLUM STEEL	331	331
1322	SKELLY OIL	291	291
572	FIRESTONE TIRE & RUBBER CO	301	301
1359	STANDARD OIL OF INDIANA	291	291
303	CERRO CORP	333	333
1008	MISSION CORP	291	671
40	AMERADA PETROLEUM CORP	291	131
1359	STANDARD OIL OF INDIANA	291	291
1322	SKELLY OIL	291	291
997	CONTINENTAL OIL	291	291
40	AMERADA PETROLEUM CORP	291	131
40	AMERADA PETROLEUM CORP	291	531
28	ALLIED STORES CORP	533	531
1308	SHELL OIL CO	291	291
998	GULF OIL CORP	291	291
321	CHICAGO MILWAUKEE ST PAULRR	331	401
25	ALLIED CHEMICAL CORP	281	281
52	AMERICAN CAN CO	341	341
321	CHICAGO MILWAUKEE ST PAULRR	451	401
825	JOHNSMANVILLE	326	326
997	CONTINENTAL OIL	291	291
1008	MISSION CORP	291	671
863	KRESGE SS	251	533
1020	MONSANTO CO	287	281
122	ARMOUR & CO	451	201
25	ALLIED CHEMICAL CORP	281	283
7	ABBOTT LABORATORIES	281	281
31	ALLIS CHALMERS MFG CO	352	352
1308	SHELL OIL CO	291	291
790	INTERNATIONAL NICKEL	333	333
21	ALLEGHENY LUDLUM STEEL	331	331
635	GENERAL REFRACTORIES CO	331	325
1308	SHELL OIL CO	291	291
635	GENERAL REFRACTORIES CO	331	325
2	ACF INDUSTRIES INC	451	374
572	FIRESTONE TIRE & RUBBER CO	301	301
997	CONTINENTAL OIL	291	291
1181	PHILLIPS PETROLEUM	291	291
119	ARMCO STEEL CORP	331	331
635	GENERAL REFRACTORIES CO	331	325
497	DUPONT	262	281
31	ALLIS CHALMERS MFG CO	333	352
21	ALLEGHENY LUDLUM STEEL	331	331
1257	ROCKWELL STANDARD CORP	356	371

Table B-2. Market Model. Listing of Companies with Least Correlated Residuals

NO	RMIN	SEC ID		SEC ID		INDUSTRYS
1	-0.3935	380	CONSOLIDATED EDISON CO NY	195	BETHLEHEM STEEL CORP	492 331
2	-0.3009	1361	STANDARD OIL OF NEW JERSEY	11	ADMIRAL CORPORATION	291 365
3	-0.2944	1361	STANDARD OIL OF NEW JERSEY	1179	PHILIP MORRIS INC	291 211
4	-0.2611	1181	PHILLIPS PETROLEUM	629	GENERAL MOTORS	291 371
5	-0.2599	1239	REYNOLDS METALS	253	CIT FINANCIAL	333 614
6	-0.2578	1358	STANDARD OIL OF CALIF.	831	JONES & LAUGHLIN STEEL CORP	291 331
7	-0.2480	1540	US STEEL	1358	STANDARD OIL OF CALIF.	331 291
8	-0.2451	1352	SPERRY RAND CORP	848	KENNECOTT COPPER	366 333
9	-0.2281	1361	STANDARD OIL OF NEW JERSEY	508	EASTMAN KODAK	291 383
10	-0.2245	1322	SKELLY OIL	629	GENERAL MOTORS	291 371
11	-0.2240	629	GENERAL MOTORS	508	EASTMAN KODAK	371 383
12	-0.2226	1361	STANDARD OIL OF NEW JERSEY	1200	PROCTOR & GAMBLE CO	291 284
13	-0.2223	1432	TEXACO	1234	REPUBLIC STEEL CORP	291 331
14	-0.2201	629	GENERAL MOTORS	487	DOW CHEMICAL CO	371 281
15	-0.2195	1358	STANDARD OIL OF CALIF.	1234	REPUBLIC STEEL CORP	291 331
16	-0.2181	997	CONTINENTAL OIL	629	GENERAL MOTORS	291 371
17	-0.2179	1432	TEXACO	11	ADMIRAL CORPORATION	291 365
18	-0.2148	1335	SOUTHERN CO	793	INTERNATIONAL PAPER	491 262
19	-0.2100	1361	STANDARD OIL OF NEW JERSEY	623	GENERAL ELECTRIC	291 361
20	-0.2080	997	CONTINENTAL OIL	11	ADMIRAL CORPORATION	291 365
21	-0.2064	998	GULF OIL CORP	122	ARMOUR & CO	291 201
22	-0.2059	1359	STANDARD OIL OF INDIANA	623	GENERAL ELECTRIC	291 361
23	-0.2058	1432	TEXACO	863	KRESGE SS	291 533
24	-0.2057	790	INTERNATIONAL NICKEL	629	GENERAL MOTORS	333 371
25	-0.2049	806	INTERNATIONAL TEL & TEL	629	GENERAL MOTORS	366 371
26	-0.2048	1008	MISSION CORP	629	GENERAL MOTORS	671 371
27	-0.2046	1361	STANDARD OIL OF NEW JERSEY	1242	REYNOLDS TOBACCO	291 211
28	-0.2044	1358	STANDARD OIL OF CALIF.	1305	SHARON STEEL CORP	291 331
29	-0.2038	1432	TEXACO	1099	NORTHWEST AIRLINES	291 451
30	-0.2028	724	HERCULES POWDER CO	629	GENERAL MOTORS	289 371
31	-0.2018	1359	STANDARD OIL OF INDIANA	253	CIT FINANCIAL	291 614
32	-0.1980	333	CHRYSLER CORP	70	AMERICAN HOME PRODUCTS	371 283
33	-0.1963	1308	SHELL OIL CO	508	EASTMAN KODAK	291 383
34	-0.1955	1361	STANDARD OIL OF NEW JERSEY	119	ARMCO STEEL CORP	291 331
35	-0.1946	1540	US STEEL	1008	MISSION CORP	331 671
36	-0.1944	1361	STANDARD OIL OF NEW JERSEY	1298	SEARS ROEBUCK	291 532
37	-0.1941	1540	US STEEL	1432	TEXACO	331 291
38	-0.1941	1452	TIMKEN ROLLER BEARING	1157	PENNSYLVANIA POWER & LIGHT	356 491
39	-0.1938	510	EATON MANUFACTURING CO	380	CONSOLIDATED EDISON CO NY	371 492
40	-0.1929	683	GREYHOUND CORP	629	GENERAL MOTORS	413 371
41	-0.1924	1358	STANDARD OIL OF CALIF.	195	BETHLEHEM STEEL CORP	291 331
42	-0.1911	1361	STANDARD OIL OF NEW JERSEY	1115	OTIS ELEVATOR	291 352
43	-0.1897	1358	STANDARD OIL OF CALIF.	87	AMERICAN RADIATOR CO	291 343
44	-0.1896	998	GULF OIL CORP	98	AT&T CO	291 481
45	-0.1893	1322	SKELLY OIL	1298	SEARS ROEBUCK	291 532
46	-0.1888	1531	US LINES CO NJ	497	DUPONT	441 281
47	-0.1878	1358	STANDARD OIL OF CALIF.	119	ARMCO STEEL CORP	291 331
48	-0.1860	303	CERRO CORP	253	CIT FINANCIAL	333 614
49	-0.1860	1361	STANDARD OIL OF NEW JERSEY	1335	SOUTHERN CO	291 491
50	-0.1852	782	IBM CORP	629	GENERAL MOTORS	357 371

51	-0.1848	1452	TIMKEN ROLLER BEARING	98	AT&T CO	356	481
52	-0.1846	998	GULF OIL CORP	629	GENERAL MOTORS	291	371
53	-0.1842	1308	SHELL OIL CO	641	GENERAL TELEPHONE & ELEC.	291	366
54	-0.1838	1361	STANDARD OIL OF NEW JERSEY	123	ARMSTRONG CORK CO	291	398
55	-0.1828	1089	NORFOLK & WESTERN RY	752	HOUSEHOLD FINANCE	401	614
56	-0.1806	1432	TEXACO	831	JONES & LAUGHLIN STEEL CORP	291	331
57	-0.1785	1358	STANDARD OIL OF CALIF.	11	ADMIRAL CORPORATION	291	365
58	-0.1785	1355	STANDARD BRANDS	629	GENERAL MOTORS	204	371
59	-0.1777	1352	SPERRY RAND CORP	629	GENERAL MOTORS	366	371
60	-0.1771	1242	REYNOLDS TOBACCO	497	DUPONT	211	281
61	-0.1768	1359	STANDARD OIL OF INDIANA	782	IBM CORP.	291	357
62	-0.1762	629	GENERAL MOTORS	7	ABBOTT LABORATORIES	371	283
63	-0.1751	825	JOHNSMANVILLE	629	GENERAL MOTORS	326	371
64	-0.1751	1359	STANDARD OIL OF INDIANA	11	ADMIRAL CORPORATION	291	365
65	-0.1749	1361	STANDARD OIL OF NEW JERSEY	1234	REPUBLIC STEEL CORP	291	331
66	-0.1746	1432	TEXACO	1305	SHARON STEEL CORP	291	331
67	-0.1744	661	GOODYEAR TIRE AND RUBBER	629	GENERAL MOTORS	301	371
68	-0.1738	998	GULF OIL CORP	31	ALLIS CHALMERS MFG CO	291	352
69	-0.1732	1298	SEARS ROEBUCK	1008	MISSION CORP	532	671
70	-0.1727	1157	PENNSYLVANIA POWER & LIGHT	998	GULF OIL CORP	491	291
71	-0.1719	1531	US LINES CO NJ	1115	OTIS ELEVATOR	441	352
72	-0.1718	1361	STANDARD OIL OF NEW JERSEY	651	GILLETTE CO	291	342
73	-0.1705	1540	US STEEL	1361	STANDARD OIL OF NEW JERSEY	331	291
74	-0.1703	1482	UNION CARBIDE CORP	1432	TEXACO	287	291
75	-0.1695	1432	TEXACO	825	JOHNSMANVILLE	291	326
76	-0.1695	1358	STANDARD OIL OF CALIF.	321	CHICAGO MILWAUKEE ST PAULRR	291	401
77	-0.1693	1355	STANDARD BRANDS	21	ALLEGHENY LUDLUM STEEL	204	331
78	-0.1678	1361	STANDARD OIL OF NEW JERSEY	1099	NORTHWEST AIRLINES	291	451
79	-0.1676	1432	TEXACO	623	GENERAL ELECTRIC	291	361
80	-0.1670	1432	TEXACO	31	ALLIS CHALMERS MFG CO	291	352
81	-0.1669	1179	PHILIP MORRIS INC	497	DUPONT	211	281
82	-0.1667	1358	STANDARD OIL OF CALIF.	659	GOODRICH BF	281	301
83	-0.1667	497	DUPONT	321	CHICAGO MILWAUKEE ST PAULRR	371	401
84	-0.1665	629	GENERAL MOTORS	572	FIRESTONE TIRE & RUBBER CO	371	301
85	-0.1663	1536	US RUBBER	752	HOUSEHOLD FINANCE	301	614
86	-0.1661	11	ADMIRAL CORPORATION	7	ABBOTT LABORATORIES	365	283
87	-0.1659	1322	SKELLY OIL	380	CONSOLIDATED EDISON CO NY	291	492
88	-0.1657	1298	SEARS ROEBUCK	195	BETHLEHEM STEEL CORP	532	331
89	-0.1656	1531	US LINES CO NJ	623	GENERAL ELECTRIC	441	361
90	-0.1654	998	GULF OIL CORP	510	EATON MANUFACTURING CO	292	371
91	-0.1653	282	CATERPILLAR TRACTOR CO	98	AT&T CO	352	481
92	-0.1651	195	BETHLEHEM STEEL CORP	98	AT&T CO	331	481
93	-0.1646	1432	TEXACO	629	GENERAL MOTORS	291	371
94	-0.1641	831	JONES & LAUGHLIN STEEL CORP	752	HOUSEHOLD FINANCE	331	614
95	-0.1636	806	INTERNATIONAL TEL & TEL	40	AMERADA PETROLEUM CORP	366	131
96	-0.1634	1452	TIMKEN ROLLER BEARING	752	HOUSEHOLD FINANCE	356	614
97	-0.1632	1361	STANDARD OIL OF NEW JERSEY	806	INTERNATIONAL TEL & TEL	291	366
98	-0.1629	1359	STANDARD OIL OF INDIANA	641	GENERAL TELEPHONE & ELEC.	291	366
99	-0.1621	1359	STANDARD OIL OF INDIANA	806	INTERNATIONAL TEL & TEL	291	366
100	-0.1615	1432	TEXACO	532	ENDICOTT JOHNSON CORP	291	314

Table B-3. Market Model. Listing of the 100 Sample Securities, Each Paired with the One Other Security with which its Residuals are *Most Highly* Correlated

MAXIMUM CORRELATIONS

NO	SEC ID		IND	NO	SEC ID		IND	CORR
1	2	ACF INDUSTRIES INC	374	67	1099	NORTHWEST AIRLINES	451	0.2997
2	7	ABBOTT LABORATORIES	283	63	1020	MONSANTO CO	281	0.3125
3	11	ADMIRAL CORPORATION	365	55	806	INTERNATIONAL TEL & TEL	366	0.2544
4	21	ALLEGHENY LUDLUM STEEL	331	57	831	JONES & LAUGHLIN STEEL CORP	331	0.4230
5	25	ALLIED CHEMICAL CORP	281	31	487	DOW CHEMICAL CO	281	0.3296
6	28	ALLIED STORES CORP	531	59	863	KRESGE SS	533	0.3363
7	31	ALLIS CHALMERS MFG CO	352	52	785	INTERNATIONAL HARVESTER	352	0.3119
8	40	AMERADA PETROLEUM CORP	131	90	1359	STANDARD OIL OF INDIANA	291	0.4384
9	46	AMERICAN BOSCH ARMA CORP	361	55	806	INTERNATIONAL TEL & TEL	366	0.2230
10	52	AMERICAN CAN CO	341	28	395	CONTINENTAL CAN CO INC	341	0.3269
11	70	AMERICAN HOME PRODUCTS	283	51	782	IBM CORP	357	0.2821
12	87	AMERICAN RADIATOR CO	343	84	1316	SIMMONS CO	251	0.2071
13	98	AT&T CO	481	41	641	GENERAL TELEPHONE & ELEC.	366	0.2053
14	119	ARMCO STEEL CORP	331	100	1540	US STEEL	331	0.5456
15	122	ARMOUR & CO	201	67	1099	NORTHWEST AIRLINES	451	0.3155
16	123	ARMSTRONG CORK CO	398	51	782	IBM CORP	357	0.2476
17	142	ATLAS CHEMICAL INDUSTRIES	289	33	508	EASTMAN KODAK	383	0.2524
18	195	BETHLEHEM STEEL CORP	331	100	1540	US STEEL	331	0.5858
19	249	BURROUGHS CORP	357	87	1352	SPERRY RAND CORP	366	0.2699
20	253	CIT FINANCIAL	614	50	752	HOUSEHOLD FINANCE	614	0.2364
21	282	CATERPILLAR TRACTOR CO	352	56	825	JOHNSMANVILLE	326	0.2419
22	286	CELANESE CORP OF AMERICA	281	6	28	ALLIED STORES CORP	531	0.2713
23	303	CERRO CORP	333	73	1176	PHELPS DODGE	333	0.3555
24	321	CHICAGO MILWAUKEE ST PAULRR	401	57	831	JONES & LAUGHLIN STEEL CORP	331	0.3306
25	333	CHRYSLER CORP	371	39	629	GENERAL MOTORS	371	0.3775
26	344	CITY STORES CO	531	6	28	ALLIED STORES CORP	531	0.2777
27	380	CONSOLIDATED EDISON CO NY	492	13	98	AT&T CO	481	0.1899
28	395	CONTINENTAL CAN CO INC	341	10	52	AMERICAN CAN CO	341	0.3269
29	426	CROWN ZELLERBACH CORP	262	54	793	INTERNATIONAL PAPER	262	0.4632
30	451	DEERE & CO	352	52	785	INTERNATIONAL HARVESTER	352	0.3666
31	487	DOW CHEMICAL CO	281	63	1020	MONSANTO CO	281	0.4591
32	497	DUPONT	281	5	25	ALLIED CHEMICAL CORP	281	0.3153
33	508	EASTMAN KODAK	383	47	724	HERCULES POWDER CO	289	0.2873
34	510	EATON MANUFACTURING CO	371	24	321	CHICAGO MILWAUKEE ST PAULRR	401	0.1946
35	532	ENDICOTT JOHNSON CORP	314	59	863	KRESGE SS	533	0.2567
36	572	FIRESTONE TIRE & RUBBER CO	301	44	661	GOODYEAR TIRE AND RUBBER	301	0.5343
37	574	FIRST NATIONAL STORES INC	541	54	793	INTERNATIONAL PAPER	262	0.2497
38	623	GENERAL ELECTRIC	361	49	745	HONEYWELL INC	381	0.2273
39	629	GENERAL MOTORS	371	25	333	CHRYSLER CORP	371	0.3775
40	635	GENERAL REFRACTORIES CO	325	57	831	JONES & LAUGHLIN STEEL CORP	331	0.3061
41	641	GENERAL TELEPHONE & ELEC.	366	69	1143	PARKE DAVIS	283	0.2056
42	651	GILLETTE CO	342	70	1157	PENNSYLVANIA POWER & LIGHT	491	0.2154
43	659	GOODRICH BF	301	44	661	GOODYEAR TIRE AND RUBBER	301	0.4439
44	661	GOODYEAR TIRE AND RUBBER	301	36	572	FIRESTONE TIRE & RUBBER CO	301	0.5343
45	683	GREYHOUND CORP	413	35	532	ENDICOTT JOHNSON CORP	314	0.2276
46	721	HELME PRODUCTS INC	213	74	1179	PHILIP MORRIS INC	211	0.2616
47	724	HERCULES POWDER CO	289	33	508	EASTMAN KODAK	383	0.2873
48	744	HOMESTAKE MINING CO	104	28	395	CONTINENTAL CAN CO INC	341	0.2182
49	745	HONEYWELL INC	381	31	487	DOW CHEMICAL CO	281	0.2766
50	752	HOUSEHOLD FINANCE	614	20	253	CIT FINANCIAL	614	0.2364

No.	ID	Firm				Associated Firm		
51	782	IBM CORP	357	11	70	AMERICAN HOME PRODUCTS	283	0.2821
52	785	INTERNATIONAL HARVESTER	352	30	451	DEERE & CO	352	0.3666
53	790	INTERNATIONAL NICKEL	333	73	1176	PHELPS DODGE	333	0.3075
54	793	INTERNATIONAL PAPER	262	29	426	CROWN ZELLERBACH CORP	262	0.4632
55	806	INTERNATIONAL TEL & TEL	326	11	11	ADMIRAL CORPORATION	365	0.2544
56	825	JOHNSMANVILLE	331	97	1527	UNITED STATES GYPSUM	326	0.3251
57	831	JONES & LAUGHLIN STEEL CORP	333	77	1234	REPUBLIC STEEL CORP	331	0.6647
58	848	KENNECOTT COPPER	533	73	1176	PHELPS DODGE	333	0.3761
59	863	KRESGE SS	291	6	28	ALLIED STORES CORP	531	0.3363
60	997	CONTINENTAL OIL	671	85	1322	SKELLY OIL	291	0.4805
61	998	GULF OIL CORP	281	89	1358	STANDARD OIL OF CALIF.	291	0.4377
62	1008	MISSION CORP	532	85	1322	SKELLY OIL	281	0.7382
63	1020	MONSANTO CO	285	31	487	DOW CHEMICAL CO	251	0.4591
64	1025	MONTGOMERY WARD	401	84	1316	SIMMONS CO	326	0.2702
65	1057	NATIONAL LEAD CO	451	56	825	JOHNSMANVILLE	352	0.2853
66	1089	NORFOLK & WESTERN RY	352	21	282	CATERPILLAR TRACTOR CO	401	0.2106
67	1099	NORTHWEST AIRLINES	283	24	321	CHICAGO MILWAUKEE ST PAULRR	326	0.3255
68	1115	OTIS ELEVATOR	491	97	1527	UNITED STATES GYPSUM	283	0.2336
69	1143	PARKE DAVIS	209	2	7	ABBOTT LABORATORIES	342	0.2765
70	1157	PENNSYLVANIA POWER & LIGHT	202	42	651	GILLETTE CO	441	0.2056
71	1165	PEPSI COLA CO	333	98	1531	US LINES CO NJ	366	0.1848
72	1169	PET MILK	211	55	806	INTERNATIONAL TEL & TEL	333	0.2171
73	1176	PHELPS DODGE	291	58	848	KENNECOTT COPPER	211	0.3761
74	1179	PHILLIP MORRIS INC	284	79	1242	REYNOLDS TOBACCO	291	0.4549
75	1181	PHILLIPS PETROLEUM	331	85	1322	SKELLY OIL	491	0.4043
76	1200	PROCTOR & GAMBLE CO	333	70	1157	PENNSYLVANIA POWER & LIGHT	331	0.1759
77	1234	REPUBLIC STEEL CORP	211	57	831	JONES & LAUGHLIN STEEL CORP	331	0.6647
78	1239	REYNOLDS METALS	371	57	831	JONES & LAUGHLIN STEEL CORP	211	0.2548
79	1242	REYNOLDS TOBACCO	532	74	1179	PHILIP MORRIS INC	356	0.4549
80	1257	ROCKWELL STANDARD CORP	331	93	1452	TIMKEN ROLLER BEARING	331	0.2897
81	1298	SEARS ROEBUCK	291	63	1020	MONSANTO CO	291	0.2156
82	1305	SHARON STEEL CORP	251	57	831	JONES & LAUGHLIN STEEL CORP	533	0.5259
83	1308	SHELL OIL CO	291	60	997	CONTINENTAL OIL	671	0.4356
84	1316	SIMMONS CO	491	59	863	KRESGE SS	614	0.3199
85	1322	SKELLY OIL	366	62	1008	MISSION CORP	357	0.7382
86	1335	SOUTHERN CO	204	20	253	CIT FINANCIAL	531	0.1849
87	1352	SPERRY RAND CORP	291	19	249	BURROUGHS CORP	291	0.2699
88	1355	STANDARD BRANDS	291	6	28	ALLIED STORES CORP	291	0.1849
89	1358	STANDARD OIL OF CALIF.	291	92	1432	TEXACO	291	0.5197
90	1359	STANDARD OIL OF INDIANA	356	60	997	CONTINENTAL OIL	371	0.4528
91	1361	STANDARD OIL OF NEW JERSEY	781	92	1432	TEXACO	202	0.4646
92	1432	TEXACO	287	89	1358	STANDARD OIL OF CALIF.	281	0.5197
93	1452	TIMKEN ROLLER BEARING	205	80	1257	ROCKWELL STANDARD CORP	211	0.2897
94	1472	TWENTIETH CENTURY FOX FILM	326	72	1169	PET MILK	326	0.2134
95	1482	UNION CARBIDE CORP	441	31	487	DOW CHEMICAL CO	201	0.4027
96	1497	UNITED BISCUIT CORP	301	74	1179	PHILIP MORRIS INC	331	0.3251
97	1527	UNITED STATES GYPSUM	331	56	825	JOHNSMANVILLE	326	0.2314
98	1531	US LINES CO NJ	441	15	122	ARMOUR & CO	201	0.2101
99	1536	US RUBBER	301	44	661	GOODYEAR TIRE AND RUBBER	301	0.3833
100	1540	US STEEL	331	57	831	JONES & LAUGHLIN STEEL CORP	331	0.5983

Table B–4. Market Model. Listing of the 100 Sample Securities, Each Paired with the One Other Security with Which its Residuals are *Least* Correlated

MINIMUM CORRELATIONS

NO	SEC ID		IND	NO	SEC ID		IND	CORR
1	2	ACF INDUSTRIES INC	374	97	1527	UNITED STATES GYPSUM	326	-0.1538
2	7	ABBOTT LABORATORIES	283	39	629	GENERAL MOTORS	371	-0.1762
3	11	ADMIRAL CORPORATION	365	91	1361	STANDARD OIL OF NEW JERSEY	291	-0.3009
4	21	ALLEGHENY LUDLUM STEEL	331	88	1355	STANDARD BRANDS	204	-0.1693
5	25	ALLIED CHEMICAL CORP	281	70	1157	PENNSYLVANIA POWER & LIGHT	491	-0.1345
6	28	ALLIED STORES CORP	531	91	1361	STANDARD OIL OF NEW JERSEY	291	-0.1310
7	31	ALLIS CHALMERS MFG CO	352	61	998	GULF OIL CORP	291	-0.1738
8	40	AMERADA PETROLEUM CORP	131	55	806	INTERNATIONAL TEL & TEL	366	-0.1636
9	46	AMERICAN BOSCH ARMA CORP	361	91	1361	STANDARD OIL OF NEW JERSEY	291	-0.1190
10	52	AMERICAN CAN CO	341	53	790	INTERNATIONAL NICKEL	333	-0.1165
11	70	AMERICAN HOME PRODUCTS	283	25	333	CHRYSLER CORP	371	-0.1980
12	87	AMERICAN RADIATOR CO	343	89	1358	STANDARD OIL OF CALIF.	291	-0.1897
13	98	AT&T CO	481	61	998	GULF OIL CORP	291	-0.1896
14	119	ARMCO STEEL CORP	331	91	1361	STANDARD OIL OF NEW JERSEY	291	-0.1955
15	122	ARMOUR & CO	201	61	998	GULF OIL CORP	291	-0.2064
16	123	ARMSTRONG CORK CO	398	91	1361	STANDARD OIL OF NEW JERSEY	291	-0.1838
17	142	ATLAS CHEMICAL INDUSTRIES	289	92	1432	TEXACO	291	-0.1268
18	195	BETHLEHEM STEEL CORP	331	27	380	CONSOLIDATED EDISON CO NY	492	-0.3935
19	249	BURROUGHS CORP	357	89	1358	STANDARD OIL OF CALIF.	291	-0.1576
20	253	CIT FINANCIAL	614	78	1239	REYNOLDS METALS	333	-0.2599
21	282	CATERPILLAR TRACTOR CO	352	13	98	AT&T CO	481	-0.1653
22	286	CELANESE CORP OF AMERICA	281	100	1540	US STEEL	331	-0.1529
23	303	CERRO CORP	333	20	253	CIT FINANCIAL	614	-0.1860
24	321	CHICAGO MILWAUKEE ST PAULRR	401	89	1358	STANDARD OIL OF CALIF.	291	-0.1695
25	333	CHRYSLER CORP	371	11	70	AMERICAN HOME PRODUCTS	283	-0.1980
26	344	CITY STORES CO	531	91	1361	STANDARD OIL OF NEW JERSEY	291	-0.1605
27	380	CONSOLIDATED EDISON CO NY	492	18	195	BETHLEHEM STEEL CORP	331	-0.3935
28	395	CONTINENTAL CAN CO INC	341	90	1359	STANDARD OIL OF INDIANA	291	-0.1108
29	426	CROWN ZELLERBACH CORP	262	39	629	GENERAL MOTORS	371	-0.1544
30	451	DEERE & CO	352	92	1432	TEXACO	291	-0.1170
31	487	DOW CHEMICAL CO	281	39	629	GENERAL MOTORS	371	-0.2201
32	497	DUPONT	281	98	1531	US LINES CO NJ	441	-0.1888
33	508	EASTMAN KODAK	383	91	1361	STANDARD OIL OF NEW JERSEY	291	-0.2281
34	510	EATON MANUFACTURING CO	371	27	380	CONSOLIDATED EDISON CO NY	492	-0.1938
35	532	ENDICOTT JOHNSON CORP	314	92	1432	TEXACO	291	-0.1615
36	572	FIRESTONE TIRE & RUBBER CO	301	39	629	GENERAL MOTORS	371	-0.1665
37	574	FIRST NATIONAL STORES INC	541	91	1361	STANDARD OIL OF NEW JERSEY	291	-0.1478
38	623	GENERAL ELECTRIC	361	91	1361	STANDARD OIL OF NEW JERSEY	291	-0.2100
39	629	GENERAL MOTORS	371	75	1181	PHILLIPS PETROLEUM	291	-0.2611
40	635	GENERAL REFRACTORIES CO	325	47	724	HERCULES POWDER CO	289	-0.1409
41	641	GENERAL TELEPHONE & ELEC.	366	83	1308	SHELL OIL CO	291	-0.1842
42	651	GILLETTE CO	342	91	1361	STANDARD OIL OF NEW JERSEY	291	-0.1718
43	659	GOODRICH BF	301	89	1358	STANDARD OIL OF CALIF.	291	-0.1667
44	661	GOODYEAR TIRE AND RUBBER	301	39	629	GENERAL MOTORS	371	-0.1744
45	683	GREYHOUND CORP	413	39	629	GENERAL MOTORS	371	-0.1929
46	721	HELME PRODUCTS INC	213	91	1361	STANDARD OIL OF NEW JERSEY	291	-0.1083
47	724	HERCULES POWDER CO	289	39	629	GENERAL MOTORS	371	-0.2028
48	744	HOMESTAKE MINING CO	104	66	1089	NORFOLK & WESTERN RY	401	-0.1611
49	745	HONEYWELL INC	381	39	629	GENERAL MOTORS	371	-0.1428
50	752	HOUSEHOLD FINANCE	614	66	1089	NORFOLK & WESTERN RY	401	-0.1828

51	782	IBM CORP	357	39	629	GENERAL MOTORS	371	-0.1852
52	785	INTERNATIONAL HARVESTER	352	13	98	AT&T CO	481	-0.1373
53	790	INTERNATIONAL NICKEL	333	39	629	GENERAL MOTORS	371	-0.2057
54	793	INTERNATIONAL PAPER	262	86	1335	SOUTHERN CO	491	-0.2148
55	806	INTERNATIONAL TEL & TEL	366	39	629	GENERAL MOTORS	371	-0.2049
56	825	JOHNSMANVILLE	326	39	629	GENERAL MOTORS	371	-0.1751
57	831	JONES & LAUGHLIN STEEL CORP	331	89	1358	STANDARD OIL OF CALIF.	291	-0.2578
58	848	KENNECOTT COPPER	333	87	1352	SPERRY RAND CORP	366	-0.2451
59	863	KRESGE SS	533	92	1432	TEXACO	291	-0.2058
60	997	CONTINENTAL OIL	291	39	629	GENERAL MOTORS	371	-0.2181
61	998	GULF OIL CORP	291	15	122	ARMOUR & CO	201	-0.2064
62	1008	MISSION CORP	671	39	629	GENERAL MOTORS	371	-0.2048
63	1020	MONSANTO CO	281	39	629	GENERAL MOTORS	371	-0.1485
64	1025	MONTGOMERY WARD	532	76	1200	PROCTOR & GAMBLE CO	284	-0.1278
65	1057	NATIONAL LEAD CO	285	39	629	GENERAL MOTORS	371	-0.1555
66	1089	NORFOLK & WESTERN RY	401	50	752	HOUSEHOLD FINANCE	614	-0.1828
67	1099	NORTHWEST AIRLINES	451	92	1432	TEXACO	291	-0.2038
68	1115	OTIS ELEVATOR	352	91	1361	STANDARD OIL OF NEW JERSEY	291	-0.1911
69	1143	PARKE DAVIS	283	39	629	GENERAL MOTORS	371	-0.1242
70	1157	PENNSYLVANIA POWER & LIGHT	491	93	1452	TIMKEN ROLLER BEARING	356	-0.1941
71	1165	PEPSI COLA CO	209	60	997	CONTINENTAL OIL	291	-0.1436
72	1169	PET MILK	202	14	119	ARMCO STEEL CORP	331	-0.1564
73	1176	PHELPS DODGE	333	41	641	GENERAL TELEPHONE & ELEC.	366	-0.1549
74	1179	PHILIP MORRIS INC	211	91	1361	STANDARD OIL OF NEW JERSEY	291	-0.2944
75	1181	PHILLIPS PETROLEUM	291	39	629	GENERAL MOTORS	371	-0.2611
76	1200	PROCTOR & GAMBLE CO	284	91	1361	STANDARD OIL OF NEW JERSEY	291	-0.2226
77	1234	REPUBLIC STEEL CORP	331	92	1432	TEXACO	291	-0.2223
78	1239	REYNOLDS METALS	333	20	253	CIT FINANCIAL	614	-0.2599
79	1242	REYNOLDS TOBACCO	211	91	1361	STANDARD OIL OF NEW JERSEY	291	-0.2046
80	1257	ROCKWELL STANDARD CORP	371	56	825	JOHNSMANVILLE	326	-0.1191
81	1298	SEARS ROEBUCK	532	91	1361	STANDARD OIL OF NEW JERSEY	291	-0.1944
82	1305	SHARON STEEL CORP	331	89	1358	STANDARD OIL OF CALIF.	291	-0.2044
83	1308	SHELL OIL CO	291	33	508	EASTMAN KODAK	383	-0.1963
84	1316	SIMMONS CO	291	38	623	GENERAL MOTORS	361	-0.1225
85	1322	SKELLY OIL	291	39	629	GENERAL ELECTRIC	371	-0.2245
86	1335	SOUTHERN CO	491	54	793	INTERNATIONAL PAPER	262	-0.2148
87	1352	SPERRY RAND CORP	366	58	848	KENNECOTT COPPER	333	-0.2451
88	1355	STANDARD BRANDS	204	39	629	GENERAL MOTORS	371	-0.1785
89	1358	STANDARD OIL OF CALIF.	291	57	831	JONES & LAUGHLIN STEEL CORP	331	-0.2578
90	1359	STANDARD OIL OF INDIANA	291	38	623	GENERAL ELECTRIC	361	-0.2059
91	1361	STANDARD OIL OF NEW JERSEY	291	3	11	ADMIRAL CORPORATION	365	-0.3009
92	1432	TEXACO	291	77	1234	REPUBLIC STEEL CORP	331	-0.2223
93	1452	TIMKEN ROLLER BEARING	356	70	1157	PENNSYLVANIA POWER & LIGHT	491	-0.1941
94	1472	TWENTIETH CENTURY FOX FILM	781	91	1361	STANDARD OIL OF NEW JERSEY	291	-0.1512
95	1482	UNION CARBIDE CORP	287	92	1432	TEXACO	291	-0.1703
96	1497	UNITED BISCUIT CO OF AMER	205	91	1361	STANDARD OIL OF NEW JERSEY	291	-0.1614
97	1527	UNITED STATES GYPSUM	326	1	1361	ACF INDUSTRIES INC	374	-0.1538
98	1531	US LINES CO NJ	441	32	497	DUPONT	281	-0.1888
99	1536	US RUBBER	301	50	752	HOUSEHOLD FINANCE	614	-0.1663
100	1540	US STEEL	331	89	1358	STANDARD OIL OF CALIF.	291	-0.2480

Table B–5. Multi-Index Model I. Listing of Companies with Most Highly Correlated Residuals

NO	RMAX	SEC ID		SEC ID		INDUSTRYS	
1	0.6973	1322	SKELLY OIL	1008	MISSION CORP	291	671
2	0.5911	1234	REPUBLIC STEEL CORP	831	JONES & LAUGHLIN STEEL CORP	331	331
3	0.5532	1540	US STEEL	831	JONES & LAUGHLIN STEEL CORP	331	331
4	0.5400	1540	US STEEL	1234	REPUBLIC STEEL CORP	331	331
5	0.5371	1540	US STEEL	195	BETHLEHEM STEEL CORP	331	331
6	0.5148	661	GOODYEAR TIRE AND RUBBER	572	FIRESTONE TIRE & RUBBER CO	301	301
7	0.5004	1540	US STEEL	119	ARMCO STEEL CORP	331	331
8	0.4783	831	JONES & LAUGHLIN STEEL CORP	195	BETHLEHEM STEEL CORP	331	331
9	0.4716	1234	REPUBLIC STEEL CORP	119	ARMCO STEEL CORP	331	331
10	0.4590	1432	TEXACO	1358	STANDARD OIL OF CALIF.	291	291
11	0.4441	1020	MONSANTO CO	487	DOW CHEMICAL CO	281	281
12	0.4354	831	JONES & LAUGHLIN STEEL CORP	119	ARMCO STEEL CORP	331	331
13	0.4303	1322	SKELLY OIL	997	CONTINENTAL OIL	291	291
14	0.4232	1242	REYNOLDS TOBACCO	1179	PHILIP MORRIS INC	211	211
15	0.4178	661	GOODYEAR TIRE AND RUBBER	659	GOODRICH BF	301	301
16	0.4163	1234	REPUBLIC STEEL CORP	195	BETHLEHEM STEEL CORP	331	331
17	0.4005	1482	UNION CARBIDE CORP	487	DOW CHEMICAL CO	287	281
18	0.3980	1305	SHARON STEEL CORP	831	JONES & LAUGHLIN STEEL CORP	331	331
19	0.3944	1322	SKELLY OIL	1308	SHELL OIL CO	291	291
20	0.3939	1359	STANDARD OIL OF INDIANA	997	CONTINENTAL OIL	291	291
21	0.3915	1358	STANDARD OIL OF CALIF.	1008	MISSION CORP	291	671
22	0.3915	629	GENERAL MOTORS	333	CHRYSLER CORP	371	371
23	0.3915	793	INTERNATIONAL PAPER	426	CROWN ZELLERBACH CORP	262	262
24	0.3847	1308	SHELL OIL CO	997	CONTINENTAL OIL	291	291
25	0.3823	1308	SHELL OIL CO	1181	PHILLIPS PETROLEUM	291	291
26	0.3785	1359	STANDARD OIL OF INDIANA	1322	SKELLY OIL	291	291
27	0.3756	1358	STANDARD OIL OF CALIF.	998	GULF OIL CORP	291	291
28	0.3717	1432	TEXACO	1008	MISSION CORP	291	671
29	0.3690	1358	STANDARD OIL OF CALIF.	1322	SKELLY OIL	291	291
30	0.3627	1536	US RUBBER	661	GOODYEAR TIRE AND RUBBER	301	301
31	0.3626	1359	STANDARD OIL OF INDIANA	40	AMERADA PETROLEUM CORP	291	131
32	0.3625	1432	TEXACO	1361	STANDARD OIL OF NEW JERSEY	291	291
33	0.3614	1359	STANDARD OIL OF INDIANA	1181	PHILLIPS PETROLEUM	291	291
34	0.3544	1008	MISSION CORP	997	CONTINENTAL OIL	671	291
35	0.3531	1181	PHILLIPS PETROLEUM	997	CONTINENTAL OIL	291	291
36	0.3503	1359	STANDARD OIL OF INDIANA	1358	STANDARD OIL OF CALIF.	291	291
37	0.3481	1322	SKELLY OIL	1181	PHILLIPS PETROLEUM	291	291
38	0.3471	1305	SHARON STEEL CORP	1234	REPUBLIC STEEL CORP	331	331
39	0.3469	1361	STANDARD OIL OF NEW JERSEY	1358	STANDARD OIL OF CALIF.	291	291
40	0.3404	1234	REPUBLIC STEEL CORP	21	ALLEGHENY LUDLUM STEEL	331	331
41	0.3375	1361	STANDARD OIL OF NEW JERSEY	1322	SKELLY OIL	291	291
42	0.3373	1361	STANDARD OIL OF NEW JERSEY	998	GULF OIL CORP	291	291
43	0.3349	1540	US STEEL	1305	SHARON STEEL CORP	331	331
44	0.3305	195	BETHLEHEM STEEL CORP	119	ARMCO STEEL CORP	331	331
45	0.3302	1536	US RUBBER	659	GOODRICH BF	301	301
46	0.3298	1176	PHELPS DODGE	848	KENNECOTT COPPER	333	333
47	0.3286	1358	STANDARD OIL OF CALIF.	997	CONTINENTAL OIL	291	291
48	0.3282	997	CONTINENTAL OIL	40	AMERADA PETROLEUM CORP	291	131
49	0.3280	1432	TEXACO	1322	SKELLY OIL	291	291
50	0.3262	1181	PHILLIPS PETROLEUM	1008	MISSION CORP	291	671
51	0.3258	659	GOODRICH BF	572	FIRESTONE TIRE & RUBBER CO	301	301
52	0.3209	831	JONES & LAUGHLIN STEEL CORP	21	ALLEGHENY LUDLUM STEEL	331	331
53	0.3185	1432	TEXACO	998	GULF OIL CORP	291	291
54	0.3182	1305	SHARON STEEL CORP	195	BETHLEHEM STEEL CORP	331	331
55	0.3147	119	ARMCO STEEL CORP	21	ALLEGHENY LUDLUM STEEL	331	331
56	0.3116	785	INTERNATIONAL HARVESTER	451	DEERE & CO	352	352
57	0.3111	395	CONTINENTAL CAN CO INC	52	AMERICAN CAN CO	341	341
58	0.3098	1322	SKELLY OIL	40	AMERADA PETROLEUM CORP	291	131
59	0.3075	497	DUPONT	25	ALLIED CHEMICAL CORP	281	281
60	0.3061	1308	SHELL OIL CO	1008	MISSION CORP	291	671

Table B-6. Multi-Index Model I. Listing of Companies with Least Correlated Residuals

NO	RMIN	SEC ID		SEC ID		INDUSTRYS	
1	-0.3747	380	CONSOLIDATED EDISON CO NY	195	BETHLEHEM STEEL CORP	492	331
2	-0.2704	1352	SPERRY RAND CORP	848	KENNECOTT COPPER	366	333
3	-0.2586	1361	STANDARD OIL OF NEW JERSEY	1200	PROCTOR & GAMBLE CO	291	284
4	-0.2501	1361	STANDARD OIL OF NEW JERSEY	1179	PHILIP MORRIS INC	291	211
5	-0.2397	11	ADMIRAL CORPORATION	2	ACF INDUSTRIES INC	365	374
6	-0.2355	1239	REYNOLDS METALS	253	CIT FINANCIAL	333	614
7	-0.2347	1242	REYNOLDS TOBACCO	825	JOHNSMANVILLE	211	326
8	-0.2334	1540	US STEEL	1008	MISSION CORP	331	671
9	-0.2323	1482	UNION CARBIDE CORP	1432	TEXACO	287	291
10	-0.2190	1335	SOUTHERN CO	321	CHICAGO MILWAUKEE ST PAULRR	491	401
11	-0.2189	629	GENERAL MOTORS	508	EASTMAN KODAK	371	383
12	-0.2160	1531	US LINES CO NJ	1115	OTIS ELEVATOR	441	352
13	-0.2158	790	INTERNATIONAL NICKEL	629	GENERAL MOTORS	333	371
14	-0.2156	333	CHRYSLER CORP	70	AMERICAN HOME PRODUCTS	371	283
15	-0.2143	998	GULF OIL CORP	629	GENERAL MOTORS	291	371
16	-0.2135	1335	SOUTHERN CO	793	INTERNATIONAL PAPER	491	262
17	-0.2096	1361	STANDARD OIL OF NEW JERSEY	623	GENERAL ELECTRIC	291	361
18	-0.2015	1352	SPERRY RAND CORP	510	EATON MANUFACTURING CO	366	371
19	-0.1998	806	INTERNATIONAL TEL & TEL	510	EATON MANUFACTURING CO	366	371
20	-0.1997	1540	US STEEL	1358	STANDARD OIL OF CALIF.	331	291
21	-0.1995	629	GENERAL MOTORS	487	DOW CHEMICAL CO	371	281
22	-0.1972	1008	MISSION CORP	831	JONES & LAUGHLIN STEEL CORP	671	331
23	-0.1955	1242	REYNOLDS TOBACCO	497	DUPONT	211	281
24	-0.1950	1472	TWENTIETH CENTURY FOX FILM	806	INTERNATIONAL TEL & TEL	781	366
25	-0.1938	1242	REYNOLDS TOBACCO	286	CELANESE CORP OF AMERICA	211	281
26	-0.1933	1181	PHILLIPS PETROLEUM	629	GENERAL MOTORS	291	371
27	-0.1917	1361	STANDARD OIL OF NEW JERSEY	752	HOUSEHOLD FINANCE	291	614
28	-0.1916	998	GULF OIL CORP	98	AT&T CO	291	481
29	-0.1905	1452	TIMKEN ROLLER BEARING	1157	PENNSYLVANIA POWER & LIGHT	356	491
30	-0.1888	1358	STANDARD OIL OF CALIF.	87	AMERICAN RADIATOR CO	291	343
31	-0.1875	1359	STANDARD OIL OF INDIANA	253	CIT FINANCIAL	291	614
32	-0.1869	724	HERCULES POWDER CO	635	GENERAL REFRACTORIES CO	289	325
33	-0.1859	1531	US LINES CO NJ	793	INTERNATIONAL PAPER	441	262
34	-0.1844	1358	STANDARD OIL OF CALIF.	831	JONES & LAUGHLIN STEEL CORP	291	331
35	-0.1843	1361	STANDARD OIL OF NEW JERSEY	1298	SEARS ROEBUCK	291	532
36	-0.1841	1057	NATIONAL LEAD CO	752	HOUSEHOLD FINANCE	285	614
37	-0.1832	721	HELME PRODUCTS INC	651	GILLETTE CO	213	342
38	-0.1826	195	BETHLEHEM STEEL CORP	11	ADMIRAL CORPORATION	331	365
39	-0.1822	1298	SEARS ROEBUCK	344	CITY STORES CO	532	531
40	-0.1818	1432	TEXACO	629	GENERAL MOTORS	291	371
41	-0.1811	782	IBM CORP	629	GENERAL MOTORS	357	371
42	-0.1799	1361	STANDARD OIL OF NEW JERSEY	119	ARMCO STEEL CORP	291	331
43	-0.1791	997	CONTINENTAL OIL	629	GENERAL MOTORS	291	371
44	-0.1790	1540	US STEEL	1322	SKELLY OIL	331	291
45	-0.1786	1540	US STEEL	286	CELANESE CORP OF AMERICA	331	281
46	-0.1783	1452	TIMKEN ROLLER BEARING	98	AT&T CO	356	481
47	-0.1765	1352	SPERRY RAND CORP	629	GENERAL MOTORS	366	371
48	-0.1747	1308	SHELL OIL CO	508	EASTMAN KODAK	291	383
49	-0.1726	1242	REYNOLDS TOBACCO	31	ALLIS CHALMERS MFG CO	211	352
50	-0.1724	1361	STANDARD OIL OF NEW JERSEY	508	EASTMAN KODAK	291	383
51	-0.1710	1157	PENNSYLVANIA POWER & LIGHT	31	ALLIS CHALMERS MFG CO	491	352
52	-0.1704	1181	PHILLIPS PETROLEUM	253	CIT FINANCIAL	291	614
53	-0.1702	1355	STANDARD BRANDS	21	ALLEGHENY LUDLUM STEEL	204	331
54	-0.1700	1361	STANDARD OIL OF NEW JERSEY	11	ADMIRAL CORPORATION	291	365
55	-0.1680	321	CHICAGO MILWAUKEE ST PAULRR	98	AT&T CO	401	481
56	-0.1679	1322	SKELLY OIL	380	CONSOLIDATED EDISON CO NY	291	492
57	-0.1668	782	IBM CORP	510	EATON MANUFACTURING CO	357	371
58	-0.1662	510	EATON MANUFACTURING CO	380	CONSOLIDATED EDISON CO NY	371	492
59	-0.1660	1165	PEPSI COLA CO	344	CITY STORES CO	209	531
60	-0.1654	87	AMERICAN RADIATOR CO	46	AMERICAN BOSCH ARMA CORP	343	361

Table B–7. Multi Index Model II. Listing of Companies with Most Highly Correlated Residuals

NO	RMAX	SEC ID		SEC ID		INDUSTRYS	
1	0.7344	1322	SKELLY OIL	1008	MISSION CORP	291	671
2	0.6502	1234	REPUBLIC STEEL CORP	831	JONES & LAUGHLIN STEEL CORP	331	331
3	0.5989	1540	US STEEL	831	JONES & LAUGHLIN STEEL CORP	331	331
4	0.5938	1540	US STEEL	1234	REPUBLIC STEEL CORP	331	331
5	0.5869	1540	US STEEL	195	BETHLEHEM STEEL CORP	331	331
6	0.5330	1540	US STEEL	119	ARMCO STEEL CORP	331	331
7	0.5271	831	JONES & LAUGHLIN STEEL CORP	195	BETHLEHEM STEEL CORP	331	331
8	0.5198	1234	REPUBLIC STEEL CORP	119	ARMCO STEEL CORP	331	331
9	0.5066	1432	TEXACO	1358	STANDARD OIL OF CALIF.	291	291
10	0.5036	661	GOODYEAR TIRE AND RUBBER	572	FIRESTONE TIRE & RUBBER CO	301	301
11	0.4861	1234	REPUBLIC STEEL CORP	195	BETHLEHEM STEEL CORP	331	331
12	0.4818	831	JONES & LAUGHLIN STEEL CORP	119	ARMCO STEEL CORP	331	331
13	0.4756	1322	SKELLY OIL	997	CONTINENTAL OIL	291	291
14	0.4686	1020	MONSANTO CO	487	DOW CHEMICAL CO	281	281
15	0.4549	1305	SHARON STEEL CORP	831	JONES & LAUGHLIN STEEL CORP	331	331
16	0.4424	793	INTERNATIONAL PAPER	426	CROWN ZELLERBACH CORP	262	262
17	0.4393	1432	TEXACO	1361	STANDARD OIL OF NEW JERSEY	291	291
18	0.4387	1359	STANDARD OIL OF INDIANA	997	CONTINENTAL OIL	291	291
19	0.4333	1359	STANDARD OIL OF INDIANA	1322	SKELLY OIL	291	291
20	0.4320	1432	TEXACO	1008	MISSION CORP	291	671
21	0.4300	1359	STANDARD OIL OF INDIANA	40	AMERADA PETROLEUM CORP	291	131
22	0.4290	1322	SKELLY OIL	1308	SHELL OIL CO	291	291
23	0.4216	1358	STANDARD OIL OF CALIF.	1008	MISSION CORP	291	671
24	0.4214	1305	SHARON STEEL CORP	1234	REPUBLIC STEEL CORP	331	331
25	0.4199	1358	STANDARD OIL OF CALIF.	998	GULF OIL CORP	291	291
26	0.4164	1308	SHELL OIL CO	997	CONTINENTAL OIL	291	291
27	0.4164	661	GOODYEAR TIRE AND RUBBER	659	GOODRICH BF	301	301
28	0.4114	1008	MISSION CORP	997	CONTINENTAL OIL	671	291
29	0.4011	1322	SKELLY OIL	40	AMERADA PETROLEUM CORP	291	131
30	0.4010	1308	SHELL OIL CO	1181	PHILLIPS PETROLEUM	291	291
31	0.3986	997	CONTINENTAL OIL	40	AMERADA PETROLEUM CORP	291	131
32	0.3958	629	GENERAL MOTORS	333	CHRYSLER CORP	371	371
33	0.3935	1482	UNION CARBIDE CORP	487	DOW CHEMICAL CO	287	281
34	0.3931	1358	STANDARD OIL OF CALIF.	1322	SKELLY OIL	291	291
35	0.3930	1242	REYNOLDS TOBACCO	1179	PHILIP MORRIS INC	211	211
36	0.3915	1361	STANDARD OIL OF NEW JERSEY	1322	SKELLY OIL	291	291
37	0.3915	1359	STANDARD OIL OF INDIANA	1358	STANDARD OIL OF CALIF.	291	291
38	0.3887	1181	PHILLIPS PETROLEUM	997	CONTINENTAL OIL	291	291
39	0.3873	1361	STANDARD OIL OF NEW JERSEY	1358	STANDARD OIL OF CALIF.	291	291
40	0.3856	1322	SKELLY OIL	1181	PHILLIPS PETROLEUM	291	291
41	0.3836	1432	TEXACO	1322	SKELLY OIL	291	291
42	0.3820	1540	US STEEL	1305	SHARON STEEL CORP	331	331
43	0.3815	195	BETHLEHEM STEEL CORP	119	ARMCO STEEL CORP	331	331
44	0.3804	1305	SHARON STEEL CORP	195	BETHLEHEM STEEL CORP	331	331
45	0.3804	1361	STANDARD OIL OF NEW JERSEY	998	GULF OIL CORP	291	291
46	0.3784	1234	REPUBLIC STEEL CORP	21	ALLEGHENY LUDLUM STEEL	331	331
47	0.3782	1432	TEXACO	998	GULF OIL CORP	291	291
48	0.3730	1359	STANDARD OIL OF INDIANA	1181	PHILLIPS PETROLEUM	291	291
49	0.3699	1358	STANDARD OIL OF CALIF.	997	CONTINENTAL OIL	291	291
50	0.3679	1008	MISSION CORP	40	AMERADA PETROLEUM CORP	671	131
51	0.3677	1181	PHILLIPS PETROLEUM	1008	MISSION CORP	291	671
52	0.3638	1536	US RUBBER	661	GOODYEAR TIRE AND RUBBER	301	301
53	0.3520	119	ARMCO STEEL CORP	21	ALLEGHENY LUDLUM STEEL	331	331
54	0.3519	1361	STANDARD OIL OF NEW JERSEY	40	AMERADA PETROLEUM CORP	291	131
55	0.3513	1308	SHELL OIL CO	1008	MISSION CORP	291	671
56	0.3500	1359	STANDARD OIL OF INDIANA	1008	MISSION CORP	291	671
57	0.3491	831	JONES & LAUGHLIN STEEL CORP	21	ALLEGHENY LUDLUM STEEL	331	331
58	0.3489	1176	PHELPS DODGE	848	KENNECOTT COPPER	333	333
59	0.3433	1432	TEXACO	1359	STANDARD OIL OF INDIANA	291	291
60	0.3410	1432	TEXACO	997	CONTINENTAL OIL	291	291
61	0.3406	1308	SHELL OIL CO	40	AMERADA PETROLEUM CORP	291	131

Table B–8. Multi Index Model II. Listing of Companies with Least Correlated Residuals

NO	RMIN	SEC ID		SEC ID		INDUSTRYS	
1	-0.4023	380	CONSOLIDATED EDISON CO NY	195	BETHLEHEM STEEL CORP	492	331
2	-0.2793	1335	SOUTHERN CO	793	INTERNATIONAL PAPER	491	262
3	-0.2703	1361	STANDARD OIL OF NEW JERSEY	623	GENERAL ELECTRIC	291	361
4	-0.2682	1352	SPERRY RAND CORP	848	KENNECOTT COPPER	366	333
5	-0.2523	1181	PHILLIPS PETROLEUM	629	GENERAL MOTORS	291	371
6	-0.2460	1540	US STEEL	1358	STANDARD OIL OF CALIF.	331	291
7	-0.2414	1358	STANDARD OIL OF CALIF.	831	JONES & LAUGHLIN STEEL CORP	291	331
8	-0.2380	1359	STANDARD OIL OF INDIANA	623	GENERAL ELECTRIC	291	361
9	-0.2378	998	GULF OIL CORP	629	GENERAL MOTORS	291	371
10	-0.2375	1361	STANDARD OIL OF NEW JERSEY	11	ADMIRAL CORPORATION	291	365
11	-0.2337	1242	REYNOLDS TOBACCO	825	JOHNSMANVILLE	211	326
12	-0.2328	1361	STANDARD OIL OF NEW JERSEY	508	EASTMAN KODAK	291	383
13	-0.2295	997	CONTINENTAL OIL	629	GENERAL MOTORS	291	371
14	-0.2253	1432	TEXACO	629	GENERAL MOTORS	291	371
15	-0.2250	1540	US STEEL	1008	MISSION CORP	331	671
16	-0.2250	1239	REYNOLDS METALS	253	CIT FINANCIAL	333	614
17	-0.2232	1361	STANDARD OIL OF NEW JERSEY	1179	PHILIP MORRIS INC	291	211
18	-0.2189	1531	US LINES CO NJ	1115	OTIS ELEVATOR	441	352
19	-0.2158	1358	STANDARD OIL OF CALIF.	1234	REPUBLIC STEEL CORP	291	331
20	-0.2118	629	GENERAL MOTORS	508	EASTMAN KODAK	371	383
21	-0.2116	1482	UNION CARBIDE CORP	1432	TEXACO	287	291
22	-0.2088	11	ADMIRAL CORPORATION	2	ACF INDUSTRIES INC	365	374
23	-0.2073	1322	SKELLY OIL	629	GENERAL MOTORS	291	371
24	-0.2023	1308	SHELL OIL CO	508	EASTMAN KODAK	291	383
25	-0.2000	333	CHRYSLER CORP	70	AMERICAN HOME PRODUCTS	371	283
26	-0.1985	1432	TEXACO	1234	REPUBLIC STEEL CORP	291	331
27	-0.1980	1242	REYNOLDS TOBACCO	497	DUPONT	211	281
28	-0.1976	510	EATON MANUFACTURING CO	380	CONSOLIDATED EDISON CO NY	371	492
29	-0.1962	1361	STANDARD OIL OF NEW JERSEY	1298	SEARS ROEBUCK	291	532
30	-0.1955	1361	STANDARD OIL OF NEW JERSEY	1200	PROCTOR & GAMBLE CO	291	284
31	-0.1940	629	GENERAL MOTORS	487	DOW CHEMICAL CO	371	281
32	-0.1936	790	INTERNATIONAL NICKEL	629	GENERAL MOTORS	333	371
33	-0.1934	1008	MISSION CORP	831	JONES & LAUGHLIN STEEL CORP	671	331
34	-0.1924	1540	US STEEL	286	CELANESE CORP OF AMERICA	331	281
35	-0.1918	1358	STANDARD OIL OF CALIF.	195	BETHLEHEM STEEL CORP	291	331
36	-0.1909	1358	STANDARD OIL OF CALIF.	629	GENERAL MOTORS	291	371
37	-0.1903	1361	STANDARD OIL OF NEW JERSEY	629	GENERAL MOTORS	291	371
38	-0.1894	1008	MISSION CORP	629	GENERAL MOTORS	671	371
39	-0.1882	724	HERCULES POWDER CO	629	GENERAL MOTORS	289	371
40	-0.1869	1432	TEXACO	623	GENERAL ELECTRIC	291	361
41	-0.1864	997	CONTINENTAL OIL	11	ADMIRAL CORPORATION	291	365
42	-0.1839	1452	TIMKEN ROLLER BEARING	1352	SPERRY RAND CORP	356	366
43	-0.1820	1358	STANDARD OIL OF CALIF.	623	GENERAL ELECTRIC	291	361
44	-0.1816	629	GENERAL MOTORS	7	ABBOTT LABORATORIES	371	283
45	-0.1814	1176	PHELPS DODGE	744	HOMESTAKE MINING CO	333	104
46	-0.1799	1540	US STEEL	1432	TEXACO	331	291
47	-0.1796	1242	REYNOLDS TOBACCO	286	CELANESE CORP OF AMERICA	211	281
48	-0.1795	1527	UNITED STATES GYPSUM	635	GENERAL REFRACTORIES CO	326	325
49	-0.1782	1531	US LINES CO NJ	11	ADMIRAL CORPORATION	441	365
50	-0.1778	1361	STANDARD OIL OF NEW JERSEY	119	ARMCO STEEL CORP	291	331
51	-0.1772	1242	REYNOLDS TOBACCO	31	ALLIS CHALMERS MFG CO	211	352
52	-0.1769	1531	US LINES CO NJ	659	GOODRICH BF	441	301
53	-0.1762	1169	PET MILK	119	ARMCO STEEL CORP	202	331
54	-0.1756	1531	US LINES CO NJ	793	INTERNATIONAL PAPER	441	262
55	-0.1751	1358	STANDARD OIL OF CALIF.	119	ARMCO STEEL CORP	291	331
56	-0.1749	998	GULF OIL CORP	31	ALLIS CHALMERS MFG CO	291	352
57	-0.1748	1322	SKELLY OIL	623	GENERAL ELECTRIC	291	361
58	-0.1743	806	INTERNATIONAL TEL & TEL	40	AMERADA PETROLEUM CORP	366	131
59	-0.1740	1358	STANDARD OIL OF CALIF.	1305	SHARON STEEL CORP	291	331
60	-0.1736	303	CERRO CORP	253	CIT FINANCIAL	333	614
61	-0.1720	1355	STANDARD BRANDS	1305	SHARON STEEL CORP	204	331

Table B–9. Multi-Index Model III. Listing of Companies with Most Highly Correlated Residuals

NO	RMAX	SEC ID		SEC ID		INDUSTRYS	
1	0.5163	1322	SKELLY OIL	1008	MISSION CORP	291	671
2	0.4473	1242	REYNOLDS TOBACCO	1179	PHILIP MORRIS INC	211	211
3	0.4160	793	INTERNATIONAL PAPER	426	CROWN ZELLERBACH CORP	262	262
4	0.3549	1540	US STEEL	119	ARMCO STEEL CORP	331	331
5	0.3405	629	GENERAL MOTORS	333	CHRYSLER CORP	371	371
6	0.3308	395	CONTINENTAL CAN CO INC	52	AMERICAN CAN CO	341	341
7	0.3251	1020	MONSANTO CO	487	DOW CHEMICAL CO	281	281
8	0.3241	1234	REPUBLIC STEEL CORP	831	JONES & LAUGHLIN STEEL CORP	331	331
9	0.3152	863	KRESGE SS	28	ALLIED STORES CORP	533	531
10	0.3098	661	GOODYEAR TIRE AND RUBBER	572	FIRESTONE TIRE & RUBBER CC	301	301
11	0.3085	1482	UNION CARBIDE CORP	487	DOW CHEMICAL CO	287	281
12	0.3054	1540	US STEEL	195	BETHLEHEM STEEL CORP	331	331
13	0.3048	1540	US STEEL	1234	REPUBLIC STEEL CORP	331	331
14	0.3022	1234	REPUBLIC STEEL CORP	119	ARMCO STEEL CORP	331	331
15	0.2931	1432	TEXACO	1358	STANDARD OIL OF CALIF.	291	291
16	0.2822	1527	UNITED STATES GYPSUM	825	JOHNSMANVILLE	326	326
17	0.2757	497	DUPONT	25	ALLIED CHEMICAL CORP	281	281
18	0.2713	1316	SIMMONS CO	863	KRESGE SS	251	533
19	0.2706	793	INTERNATIONAL PAPER	497	DUPONT	262	281
20	0.2696	1143	PARKE DAVIS	7	ABBOTT LABORATORIES	283	283
21	0.2688	1020	MONSANTO CO	7	ABBOTT LABORATORIES	281	283
22	0.2657	1540	US STEEL	831	JONES & LAUGHLIN STEEL CORP	331	331
23	0.2544	451	DEERE & CO	40	AMERADA PETROLEUM CORP	352	131
24	0.2497	1527	UNITED STATES GYPSUM	1057	NATIONAL LEAD CO	326	285
25	0.2480	793	INTERNATIONAL PAPER	574	FIRST NATIONAL STORES INC	262	541
26	0.2452	1352	SPERRY RAND CORP	249	BURROUGHS CORP	366	357
27	0.2427	344	CITY STORES CO	28	ALLIED STORES CORP	531	531
28	0.2413	782	IBM CORP	70	AMERICAN HOME PRODUCTS	357	283
29	0.2412	683	GREYHOUND CORP	70	AMERICAN HOME PRODUCTS	413	283
30	0.2407	1179	PHILIP MORRIS INC	721	HELME PRODUCTS INC	211	213
31	0.2314	1452	TIMKEN ROLLER BEARING	1257	ROCKWELL STANDARD CORP	356	371
32	0.2261	806	INTERNATIONAL TEL & TEL	249	BURROUGHS CORP	366	357
33	0.2253	1482	UNION CARBIDE CORP	1020	MONSANTO CO	287	281
34	0.2248	744	HOMESTAKE MINING CO	395	CONTINENTAL CAN CO INC	104	341
35	0.2236	1057	NATIONAL LEAD CO	497	DUPONT	285	281
36	0.2218	831	JONES & LAUGHLIN STEEL CORP	119	ARMCO STEEL CORP	331	331
37	0.2213	1432	TEXACO	1361	STANDARD OIL OF NEW JERSEY	291	291
38	0.2209	1305	SHARON STEEL CORP	1157	PENNSYLVANIA POWER & LIGHT	331	491
39	0.2206	782	IBM CORP	123	ARMSTRONG CORK CO	357	398
40	0.2185	1316	SIMMONS CO	1025	MONTGOMERY WARD	251	532
41	0.2176	70	AMERICAN HOME PRODUCTS	46	AMERICAN BOSCH ARMA CORP	283	361
42	0.2164	574	FIRST NATIONAL STORES INC	497	DUPONT	541	281
43	0.2157	1358	STANDARD OIL OF CALIF.	998	GULF OIL CORP	291	291
44	0.2136	863	KRESGE SS	532	ENICOTT JOHNSON CORP	533	314
45	0.2134	1497	UNITED BISCUIT CO OF AMER	1179	PHILIP MORRIS INC	205	211
46	0.2109	724	HERCULES POWDER CO	508	EASTMAN KODAK	289	383
47	0.2104	1057	NATIONAL LEAD CO	825	JOHNSMANVILLE	285	326
48	0.2088	785	INTERNATIONAL HARVESTER	451	DEERE & CO	352	352
49	0.2085	40	AMERADA PETROLEUM CORP	2	ACF INDUSTRIES INC	131	374
50	0.2051	1359	STANDARD OIL OF INDIANA	40	AMERADA PETROLEUM CORP	291	131
51	0.2047	831	JONES & LAUGHLIN STEEL CORP	195	BETHLEHEM STEEL CORP	331	331
52	0.2032	782	IBM CORP	683	GREYHOUND CORP	357	413
53	0.2020	1335	SOUTHERN CO	253	CIT FINANCIAL	491	614
54	0.2007	1176	PHELPS DODGE	848	KENNECOTT COPPER	333	333
55	0.1991	1157	PENNSYLVANIA POWER & LIGHT	651	GILLETTE CO	491	342
56	0.1981	782	IBM CORP	508	EASTMAN KODAK	357	383
57	0.1980	744	HOMESTAKE MINING CO	253	CIT FINANCIAL	104	614
58	0.1972	1482	UNION CARBIDE CORP	497	DUPONT	287	281
59	0.1957	1527	UNITED STATES GYPSUM	793	INTERNATIONAL PAPER	326	262
60	0.1956	1335	SOUTHERN CO	7	ABBOTT LABORATORIES	491	283
61	0.1945	683	GREYHOUND CORP	661	GOODYEAR TIRE AND RUBBER	413	301

Table B-10. Multi-Index Model III. Listing of Companies with Least Correlated Residuals

NO	RMIN	SEC ID		SEC ID		INDUSTRYS	
1	-0.4300	380	CONSOLIDATED EDISON CO NY	195	BETHLEHEM STEEL CORP	492	331
2	-0.2852	806	INTERNATIONAL TEL & TEL	629	GENERAL MOTORS	366	371
3	-0.2736	1239	REYNOLDS METALS	1176	PHELPS DODGE	333	333
4	-0.2705	1352	SPERRY RAND CORP	848	KENNECOTT COPPER	366	333
5	-0.2399	1361	STANDARD OIL OF NEW JERSEY	1200	PROCTOR & GAMBLE CO	291	284
6	-0.2384	1361	STANDARD OIL OF NEW JERSEY	1179	PHILIP MORRIS INC	291	211
7	-0.2292	1335	SOUTHERN CO	629	GENERAL MOTORS	491	371
8	-0.2237	1531	US LINES CO NJ	1115	OTIS ELEVATOR	441	352
9	-0.2196	782	IBM CORP	629	GENERAL MOTORS	357	371
10	-0.2188	806	INTERNATIONAL TEL & TEL	333	CHRYSLER CORP	366	371
11	-0.2179	1020	MONSANTO CO	142	ATLAS CHEMICAL INDUSTRIES	281	289
12	-0.2122	1452	TIMKEN ROLLER BEARING	1157	PENNSYLVANIA POWER & LIGHT	356	491
13	-0.2106	1179	PHILIP MORRIS INC	497	DUPONT	211	281
14	-0.2080	510	EATON MANUFACTURING CO	380	CONSOLIDATED EDISON CO NY	371	492
15	-0.2038	1335	SOUTHERN CO	793	INTERNATIONAL PAPER	491	262
16	-0.2032	1358	STANDARD OIL OF CALIF.	87	AMERICAN RADIATOR CO	291	343
17	-0.2021	641	GENERAL TELEPHONE & ELEC.	572	FIRESTONE TIRE & RUBBER CO	366	301
18	-0.2009	1531	US LINES CO NJ	659	GOODRICH BF	441	301
19	-0.2002	1242	REYNOLDS TOBACCO	497	DUPONT	211	281
20	-0.1996	1536	US RUBBER	752	HOUSEHOLD FINANCE	301	614
21	-0.1991	1361	STANDARD OIL OF NEW JERSEY	1242	REYNOLDS TOBACCO	291	211
22	-0.1977	1115	OTIS ELEVATOR	451	DEERE & CO	352	352
23	-0.1967	1239	REYNOLDS METALS	253	CIT FINANCIAL	333	614
24	-0.1964	1242	REYNOLDS TOBACCO	825	JOHNSMANVILLE	211	326
25	-0.1953	1355	STANDARD BRANDS	629	GENERAL MOTORS	204	371
26	-0.1951	1115	OTIS ELEVATOR	629	GENERAL MOTORS	352	371
27	-0.1949	333	CHRYSLER CORP	70	AMERICAN HOME PRODUCTS	371	283
28	-0.1933	629	GENERAL MOTORS	98	AT&T CO	371	481
29	-0.1928	1020	MONSANTO CO	11	ADMIRAL CORPORATION	281	365
30	-0.1914	683	GREYHOUND CORP	629	GENERAL MOTORS	413	371
31	-0.1911	806	INTERNATIONAL TEL & TEL	510	EATON MANUFACTURING CO	366	371
32	-0.1909	1432	TEXACO	863	KRESGE SS	291	533
33	-0.1906	1308	SHELL OIL CC	508	EASTMAN KODAK	291	383
34	-0.1900	1361	STANDARD OIL OF NEW JERSEY	651	GILLETTE CO	291	342
35	-0.1887	11	ADMIRAL CORPORATION	2	ACF INDUSTRIES INC	365	374
36	-0.1886	629	GENERAL MOTORS	508	EASTMAN KODAK	371	383
37	-0.1872	1452	TIMKEN ROLLER BEARING	1335	SOUTHERN CO	356	491
38	-0.1871	1089	NORFOLK & WESTERN RY	752	HOUSEHOLD FINANCE	401	614
39	-0.1845	532	ENDICOTT JOHNSON CORP	282	CATERPILLAR TRACTOR CO	314	352
40	-0.1806	1057	NATIONAL LEAD CO	752	HOUSEHOLD FINANCE	285	614
41	-0.1794	1361	STANDARD OIL OF NEW JERSEY	11	ADMIRAL CORPORATION	291	365
42	-0.1780	1099	NORTHWEST AIRLINES	1057	NATIONAL LEAD CO	451	285
43	-0.1780	1452	TIMKEN ROLLER BEARING	98	AT&T CO	356	481
44	-0.1777	1298	SEARS ROEBUCK	629	GENERAL MOTORS	532	371
45	-0.1777	1531	US LINES CO NJ	793	INTERNATIONAL PAPER	441	262
46	-0.1776	1355	STANDARD BRANDS	745	HONEYWELL INC	204	381
47	-0.1768	321	CHICAGO MILWAUKEE ST PAULRR	25	ALLIED CHEMICAL CORP	401	281
48	-0.1766	785	INTERNATIONAL HARVESTER	752	HOUSEHOLD FINANCE	352	614
49	-0.1765	1020	MONSANTO CO	344	CITY STORES CO	281	531
50	-0.1750	724	HERCULES POWDER CO	11	ADMIRAL CORPORATION	289	365
51	-0.1748	487	DOW CHEMICAL CO	142	ATLAS CHEMICAL INDUSTRIES	281	289
52	-0.1746	1527	UNITED STATES GYPSUM	1099	NORTHWEST AIRLINES	326	451
53	-0.1744	1361	STANDARD OIL OF NEW JERSEY	344	CITY STORES CO	291	531
54	-0.1738	1169	PET MILK	282	CATERPILLAR TRACTOR CO	202	352
55	-0.1732	1257	ROCKWELL STANDARD CORP	46	AMERICAN BOSCH ARMA CORP	371	361
56	-0.1732	1234	REPUBLIC STEEL CORP	790	INTERNATIONAL NICKEL	331	333
57	-0.1731	1143	PARKE DAVIS	785	INTERNATIONAL HARVESTER	283	352
58	-0.1718	1057	NATIONAL LEAD CO	635	GENERAL REFRACTORIES CO	285	325
59	-0.1707	1452	TIMKEN ROLLER BEARING	651	GILLETTE CO	356	342
60	-0.1694	1452	TIMKEN ROLLER BEARING	752	HOUSEHOLD FINANCE	356	614
61	-0.1673	1361	STANDARD OIL OF NEW JERSEY	1115	OTIS ELEVATOR	291	352

Appendix C

Portfolio Volatility for the Sample Mutual
Funds Plotted with Levels of the Standard &
Poor's 500 Composite Index 1959–1970

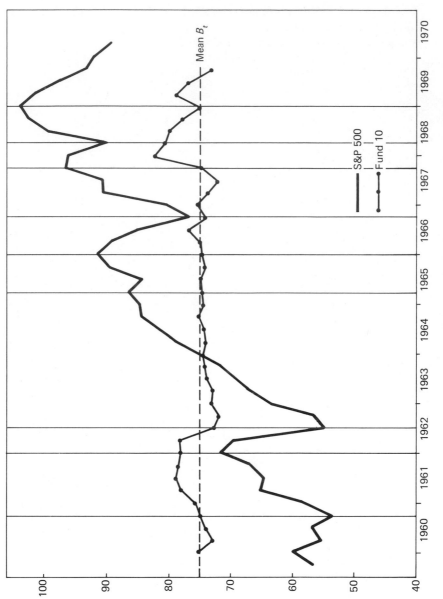

Figure C-1. Levels of Portfolio Volatility for Fund 10.

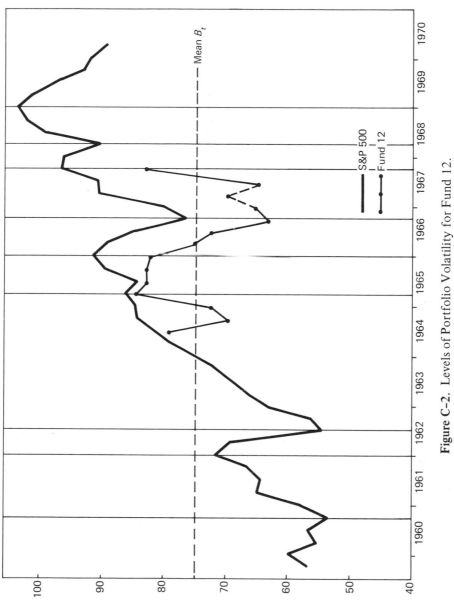

Figure C-2. Levels of Portfolio Volatility for Fund 12.

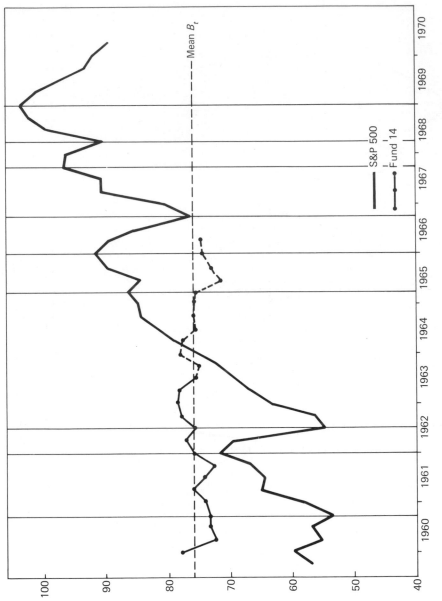

Figure C-3. Levels of Portfolio Volatility for Fund 14.

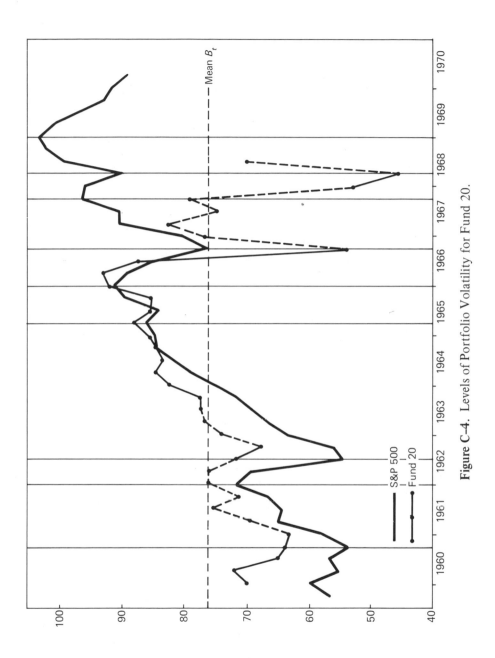

Figure C-4. Levels of Portfolio Volatility for Fund 20.

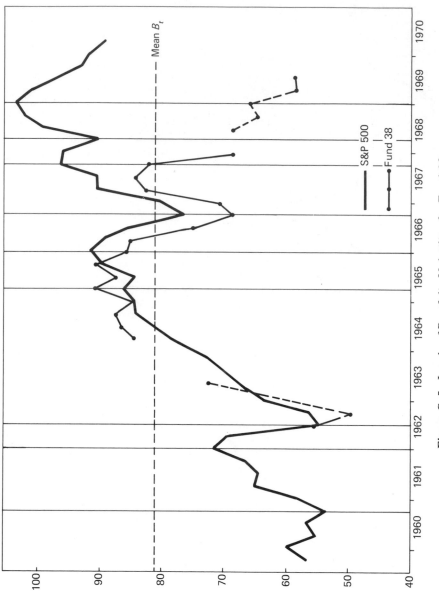

Figure C-5. Levels of Portfolio Volatility for Fund 38.

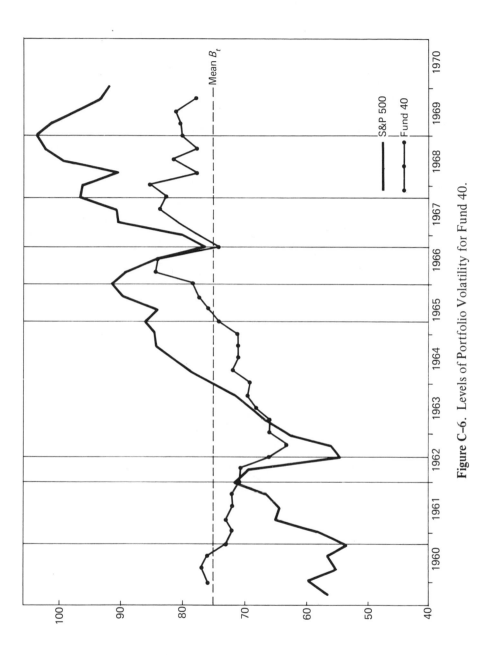

Figure C-6. Levels of Portfolio Volatility for Fund 40.

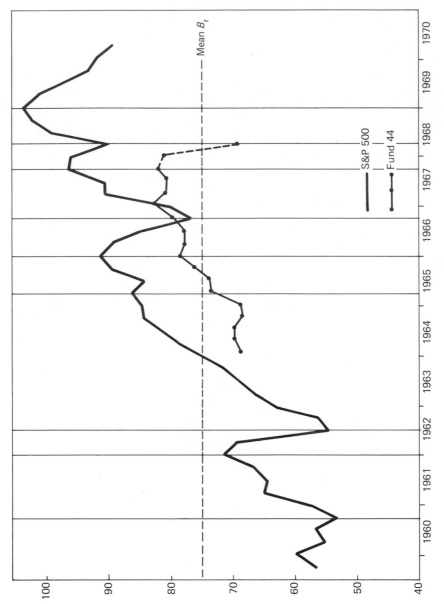

Figure C-7. Levels of Portfolio Volatility for Fund 44.

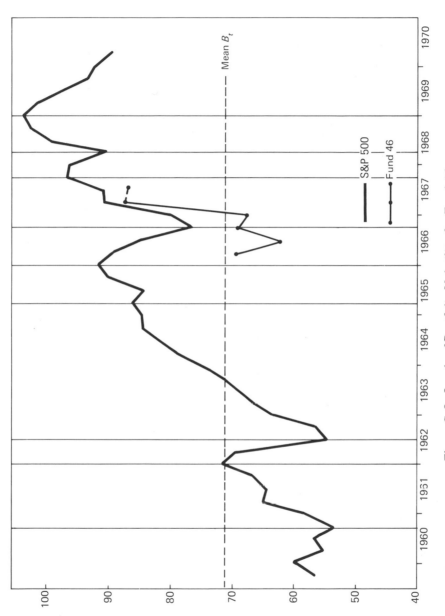

Figure C–8. Levels of Portfolio Volatility for Fund 46.

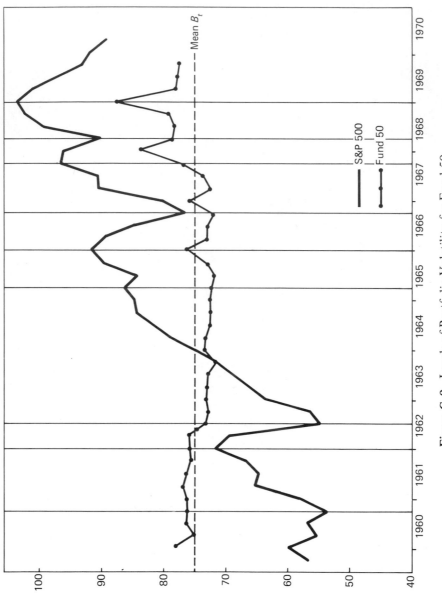

Figure C-9. Levels of Portfolio Volatility for Fund 50.

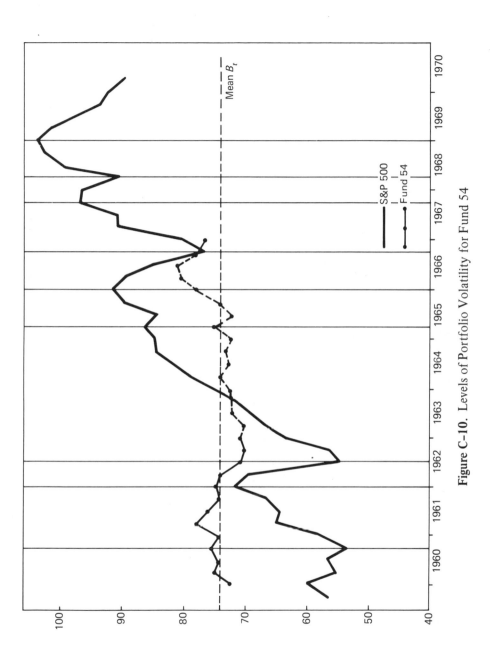

Figure C-10. Levels of Portfolio Volatility for Fund 54

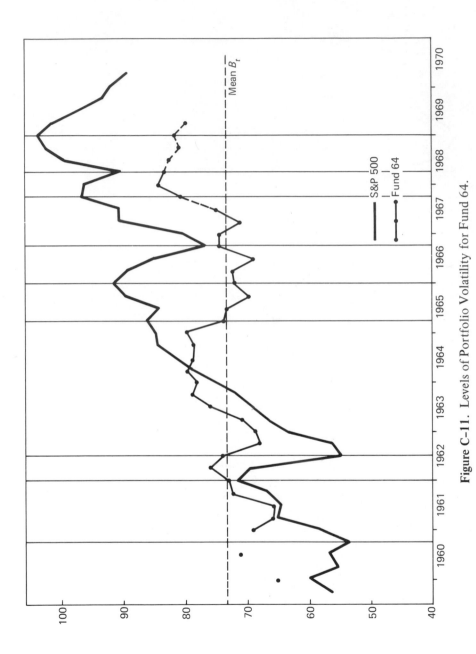

Figure C-11. Levels of Portfolio Volatility for Fund 64.

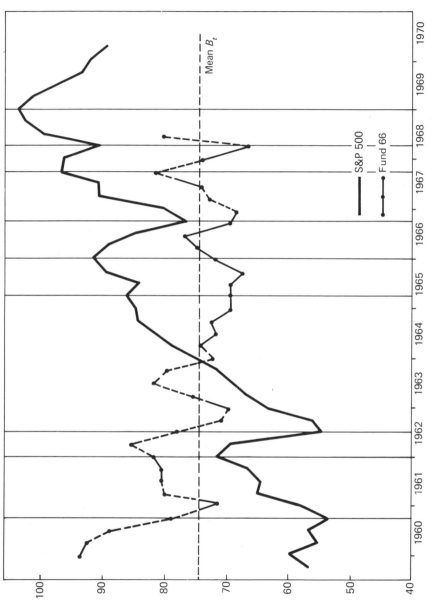

Figure C-12. Levels of Portfolio Volatility for Fund 66.

Bibliography

Arditti, Fred D. "Risk and the Required Return on Equity." *Journal of Finance* XXII (March 1967): 19–36.

Blume, Marshall. "Portfolio Theory: A Step Toward Its Practical Application." *Journal of Business* XLIII, no. 2 (April 1970): 152–173.

Campanella, Frank B. "An Investigation of the Economic and Financial Variables That Influence Mutual Fund Industry Sales and Redemptions." Unpublished report for the Investment Company Institute, December 1970.

Carlson, Robert S. "Aggregate Performance of Mutual Funds, 1948–1967." *Journal of Financial and Quantitative Analysis,* V, no. 1 (March 1970): 1–32.

Clarkson, G. P. E. "A Model of Trust Investment Behavior." Reprinted in Cohen & Hammer, *Analytical Methods in Banking.* Homewood, Ill.: Richard Irwin, 1966. Pp. 340–353.

Cohen, K. J., and J. A. Pogue. "Am Empirical Evaluation of Alternative Portfolio Selection Models." *Journal of Business* XL (April 1967): 166–193.

Cootner, Paul H., ed. *The Random Character of Stock Market Prices.* Cambridge, Mass.: MIT Press, 1964.

Dietz, Peter. *Pension Funds: Measuring Investment Performance.* New York: Free Press, 1966.

Fama, Eugene F. "Portfolio Analysis in a Stable Paretian Market." *Management Science* XI (January 1965): 404–419.

——. "Risk, Return and Equilibrium, Some Clarifying Comments. *Journal of Finance* XXIII, no. 1 (March 1968): 29–40.

Farrar, Donald E. *The Investment Decision Under Uncertainty.* Englewood Cliffs, N.J.: Prentice–Hall, 1962.

Fisher, Lawrence. "Some New Stock Market Indexes." *Journal of Business* XXIX, no. 1, pt. II (January 1966): 191–225.

Fisher, Lawrence, and J. H. Lorie. "Rates of Return on Investment in Common Stocks." *Journal of Business* (January 1964 and July 1968).

Friedman, Milton, and L. J. Savage. "The Utility Analysis of Choices Involving Risk." *Journal of Political Economy* LVI (August 1948): 279–304.

Friend, I., and D. Vickers, "Portfolio Selection and Investment Performance." *Journal of Finance* XX (September 1965): 391–415.

——. "Reevaluation of Alternative Portfolio Selection Models." *Journal of Business* XLI (April 1968): 174–179.

Friend, I., M. Blume, and Jean Crockett. *Mutual Funds and Other Institutional Investors: A New Perspective.* New York: McGraw-Hill, 1970.

Glauber, Robert R. Seminar in the Quantitative Analysis of Investment Portfolio Decisions. Unpublished notes, Harvard University Graduate School of Business, 1969.

Horowitz, Ira. "The Reward to Variability Ratio and Mutual Fund Performance." *Journal of Business* XXXIX (October 1966): 485–488.

Jensen, Michael C. "The Performance of Mutual Funds in the Period 1945–1964."
    Journal of Finance XXIII, no. 2 (May 1968): 389–419.
——. "Risk, the Pricing of Capital Assets, and the Evaluation of Investment
    Portfolios." *Journal of Business* XLII, no. 2 (April 1969): 167–247.
Johnston, J. *Econometric Methods.* New York: McGraw-Hill, 1963.
King, Benjamin F. "Market and Industry Factors in Stock Price Behavior."
    Journal of Business XXXIX, no. 1, pt. II (January 1966): 139–190.
Lintner, John. "Security Prices, Risk, and Maximal Gains from Diversification."
    Journal of Finance XX, no. 4 (December 1965): 587–616.
——. "The Valuation of Risk Assets and the Selection of Risky Investments in
    Stock Portfolios and Capital Budgets." *Review of Economics and Statistics*
    LXVII (February 1965): 13–37.
Mao, James, and C. D. Sarndal. "A Decision Theory Approach to Portfolio
    Selection." *Management Science* XII, no. 8 (April 1966): 323–333.
Markowitz, Harry M., "Portfolio Selection." *Journal of Finance* VII (March
    1952): 77–91.
——. *Portfolio Selection: Efficient Diversification of Investments.* New York:
    Wiley, 1959.
Morrison, Donald F. *Multivariate Statistical Methods.* New York: McGraw-Hill,
    1967.
Mossin, Jan. "Optimal Multi-Period Portfolio Analysis." *Journal of Business*
    XLI, no. 2 (April 1968): 221–223.
Osborne, M. F. M. "Brownian Motion in the Stock Market." *Operations Research*
    (March-April 1959).
Pearson, E. S., and H. O. Hartley. *Biometrika Tables for Statisticians,* Vol. 1.
    Cambridge, England: University Press, 1966.
Pratt, J. W. "Risk Aversion in the Small and in the Large." *Econometrika* XXXII
    (January-April, 1964): 122–136.
Pratt, J. W., H. Raiffa, and R. Schlaifer. *Introduction to Statistical Decision
    Theory.* New York: McGraw-Hill, 1965.
Sharpe, William F. "A Simplified Model for Portfolio Analysis." *Management
    Science* IX, no. 2 (January 1963): 277–293.
——. "Capital Asset Prices: A Theory of Market Equilibrium Under Conditions
    of Risk." *Journal of Finance* XIX (September 1964): 425–442.
——. "Risk Aversion in the Stock Market: Some Empirical Evidence." *Journal of
    Finance* XX (September 1965): 416–422
——. "Mutual Fund Performance." *Journal of Business* XXXIX, no. 1, pt. II
    (January 1966): 119–138.
——. "Security Prices, Risk, and Maximal Gains from Diversification: Reply."
    Journal of Finance XXI (December 1966): 743–744.
Tobin, James. "Liquidity Preference as Behavior Toward Risk." *Review of Eco-
    nomic Studies* XXV (February 1958): 65–86.
Treynor, J. L. "How to Rate Management of Investment Funds." *Harvard
    Business Review* XLIII (January-February 1965): 63–75.
Treynor, J. L., and K. K. Mazuy, "Can Mutual Funds Outguess the Market."
    Harvard Business Review XLIV (July-August 1966): 131–136.

Treynor, J. L., William W. Priest, Jr., Lawrence Fisher, and Catherine A. Higgins. "Using Portfolio Composition to Estimate Risk." *Financial Analysts Journal* XXIV (September-October 1968): 93–100.

Wiesenberger, Arthur. *Investment Companies.* New York: Arthur Wiesenberger & Co., 1960, 1968, 1969.

About the Author

Frank B. Campanella. Prior to joining the School of Management faculty at Boston College, Dr. Campanella was awarded the D.B.A. at the Harvard Business School where he participated in research dealing with aggregate performance of mutual funds and with the development of portfolio risk exposure models. He received the M.B.A., with highest distinction, from Babson College and a B.S. from Rensselaer Polytechnic Institute. His background includes work in engineering and also as Treasurer of a small corporation. In 1971 he completed a study for the Investment Company Institute, which examined the economic and financial variables that affect aggregate funds flows within the mutual fund industry. He is also co-author of the book, *Venture Capital A Guidebook For New Enterprises,* published by the Management Institute at Boston College. He has participated in special programs designed to acquaint entrepreneurs with the venture capital process and has acted as consultant to various small businesses.